The Purpose of Physical Reality

JOHN S. HATCHER

The Purpose of Physical Reality
The Kingdom of Names

Bahá'í Publishing Trust
Wilmette, Illinois 60091

Bahá'í Publishing Trust, Wilmette, Illinois 60091

Library of Congress Cataloging-in-Publication Data

Hatcher, John, Dr.
  The purpose of physical reality.

  Bibliography: p.
  1. Bahai Faith—Doctrines. 2. Theodicy. 3. Spirituality.
4. Cosmology. I. Title.
BP370.H38 1987   297'.8924   87-1388
ISBN 0-87743-208-2

Designed by John Solarz

For my mother
Helen Hardman Hatcher
with love and appreciation

Contents

Acknowledgments

Part of my joy in becoming a Bahá'í derived from the confirmation in the Bahá'í writings that the study of religion need not be the exclusive province of theologians. In fact, Bahá'u'lláh commands each of us to immerse ourselves in the ocean of His words that we "may unravel its secrets, and discover all the pearls of wisdom that lie hid in its depths" (*Synopsis* 27). In 1973, having been a Bahá'í for a number of years, I suddenly felt that at the heart of this exhortation was a challenge for us to discern the underlying logic and wisdom pervading the laws of God and His entire creation.

Tantalized by this thought, I set out to discover the rationale behind what seemed to me the most fundamental of all questions in this life: why God in His wisdom deemed it appropriate for us as essentially spiritual beings to take our beginning in a physical environment. *The Purpose of Physical Reality* is the result of my search into the ocean depths of Bahá'u'lláh's revealed writings to discover the answer to this mystery. I hope that in this work I have managed to bring a few pearls to the surface. I have not labored under the delusion that I could discover definitive answers to a question so limitless in scope. It has been my hope, rather, that my own search might entice others into the same bountiful waters.

Because the process of my investigation has taken place over so many years, portions of *The Purpose of Physical Reality* utilize work I have previously published or given as papers. Chapter 3, originally begun in 1973 as an essay for *World Order,* was given as a paper in January 1977 at the annual meeting of the Canadian Association for Studies on the Bahá'í Faith and published the same year as volume 3 of *Bahá'í Studies,* entitled "The Metaphorical Nature of Physical Reality." The article was then revised for publication in the Summer 1977 issue of *World Order* under the same title. A condensed version, called "Life as Metaphor," was published this year in *The Bahá'í World,* volume 18. Chapter 4 draws on "Afterlife and the Twin Pillars of Education," which first appeared in *World Order* (Fall 1978) and was reprinted in 1984 in volume 11, numbers 5 and 6, of *Glory* magazine. Chapter 1 derives in part from an essay I wrote in 1982 as a submission to *Bahá'í Studies.*

The response to all of my efforts has encouraged me through the years to continue my research, as has the assistance of a number of individuals. My brother Dr. William S. Hatcher, who introduced me to the Bahá'í Faith, has shared his insights, as has my wife Lucia Corsiglia Hatcher, whose opinion about my work is always my surest guide. I also wish to express my particular appreciation for the enthusiasm of the attendees at the 1977 meeting of the Canadian Association for Studies on the Bahá'í Faith (now Association for Bahá'í Studies). That initial excitement about my work was instrumental in my continuing effort. I am likewise indebted to various Bahá'ís through the years who have told me that my essays have assisted their own study.

Finally, I am grateful to Larry Bucknell and the Bahá'í Publishing Trust for deciding to publish this work and to General Manager Terrill Hayes and Associate Editor Richard Hill for their special expertise. I am also greatly indebted to General Editor Dr. Betty J. Fisher for her keen interest in this work through the years and her fine editorial assistance in bringing this project to fruition.

JOHN S. HATCHER

The
Purpose
of
Physical
Reality

The Search for Divine Justice in the Physical World   **1**

*The essence of all that We have revealed for thee is
Justice, is for man to free himself from idle fancy and
imitation, discern with the eye of oneness His glorious
handiwork, and look into all things with a searching eye.*

—Bahá'u'lláh

In contrast to most institutionalized religions, the Bahá'í Faith
teaches that theology is logical and that we should examine our
religious beliefs with the same rational faculties and rigorous
standards with which we probe the phenomenal world. From such
a view questioning is not deemed heresy but is, rather, an essential
tool for acquiring belief.

One indication of the respect which the Bahá'í Faith has for
such independent investigation as an aid to spiritual understanding
is the fact that many of the major Bahá'í writings are answers to
questions put to the Central Figures of the religion. The Kitáb-i-Íqán
responds to "questions addressed to Bahá'u'lláh by the as yet
unconverted maternal uncle of the Báb" (Shoghi Effendi, *God
Passes By* 138). *Some Answered Questions* is 'Abdu'l-Bahá's response to questions posed by Laura Clifford Barney. Much of the
valuable guidance from Shoghi Effendi, the Guardian of the Bahá'í
Faith, and from the Universal House of Justice comes as answers to
questions submitted by individual Bahá'ís. In short, one of the ways
that Bahá'ís are urged to "enter the City of Certitude" (Bahá'u'lláh,
Kitáb-i-Íqán 197) is through thoughtful study and meditation. In the
Kitáb-i-Aqdas Bahá'u'lláh commands such study when He says,
"Immerse yourselves in the ocean of My words, that ye may unravel

3

its secrets, and discover all the pearls of wisdom that lie hid in its depths'' (*Synopsis* 27).

In spite of the various exhortations in the Bahá'í writings to consider the rational basis for belief, one essential question rarely gets asked, not because it is forbidden, not because the answer is unavailable in the Bahá'í writings, but because most people probably do not think to ask it. The question concerns physical reality—why it exists and how it works. The issue is sometimes dismissed with an axiomatic but ultimately unsatisfying response: Since God fashioned the physical world, and since He has intended that we should evolve spiritually, the phenomenal world must be a benevolent creation which somehow facilitates our development. Another frequent but no less insufficient response is that our physical experience is a period of testing wherein we acquire spiritual attributes.

These answers may be true. To some of us they may be initially comforting, but they do not penetrate to our hearts, where the question is conceived in the first place. The answers hardly resolve the paradox of why essentially spiritual beings are ordained to take their beginning in a physical environment. Neither do they help us respond intelligently and effectively to a phenomenal world which often seems to make little sense.

The Bahá'í writings themselves may appear enigmatic concerning physical reality. In one Hidden Word, for example, Bahá'u'lláh admonishes us to become detached from physical things: "Abandon not the everlasting beauty for a beauty that must die, and set not your affections on this mortal world of dust" (*Hidden Words* 26). In another Hidden Word, however, Bahá'u'lláh commands us to become thoroughly involved in the physical world and even suggests that our physical actions are the most important gauge of our spiritual achievement: "The best of men are they that earn a livelihood by their calling and spend upon themselves and upon their kindred for the love of God, the Lord of all worlds" (*Hidden Words* 51).

Since there are no explicit contradictions in the writings of Bahá'u'lláh regarding physical reality, and since Bahá'u'lláh has provided us with the necessary laws and institutions to direct our temporal affairs, the question of why there is a physical reality may seem superfluous. Quite possibly this is another reason the question rarely gets asked. But the result of this unasked question remaining unanswered can sometimes be devastating. Our certitude may be shaken by the appearance of blatant injustice in a supposedly just creation, or we may become profoundly torn between the worthy goal of devoting ourselves to professional achievement and paying attention to more explicitly spiritual endeavors such as teaching and assisting others. In short, we may well come to accept a vision of ourselves as precariously tottering between two worlds, and we may approach things physical with confusion or with a vague but haunting sense of guilt or anxiety.

We may find some comfort in Bahá'u'lláh's conditional permission to enjoy the material bounties of this world: "Should a man wish to adorn himself with the ornaments of the earth, to wear its apparels, or partake of the benefits it can bestow, no harm can befall him, if he alloweth nothing whatever to intervene between him and God. . . . " (qtd. in Shoghi Effendi, *Advent* 33). But at what point does material involvement "intervene"? How do we live simultaneously in two disparate realities? Our rational and emotional dilemma is compounded by our daily experience. We sense within us two natures, one spiritual and transcendent, the other appetitive and mundane, and more often than not the fulfillment of one seems to deny fulfillment of the other.

Certainly the answer to the dilemma we face as spiritual beings in a physical environment is beyond our complete comprehension. At the same time, such a fundamental dilemma cannot remain totally unresolved without eroding to some degree our certitude and conviction. Conversely, to discover even a portion of the answer to this dilemma could greatly strengthen our resolve to use well the unique opportunities afforded by our physical experience. For if God is a wise and loving educator of His creation and could have created whatever environment for us that He wished, there must have been a very special reason He chose to have us begin an eternal spiritual journey in an environment so seemingly contrary to our lofty purposes.

The quest for an answer to our dilemma must begin by dividing the weighty matter into manageable parts. First, we can benefit from examining some previous major attempts to respond to the question and from determining how these efforts compare to the Bahá'í teachings. After establishing the fundamental problems which relate to the question of physical reality, we can delineate with some exactitude the Bahá'í paradigm or model of physical creation. Our third step in this search will then be to determine the practical implications of the paradigm—how physical experience can produce spiritual results in our daily lives. Our final part in this quest will be to approach what is perhaps the most crucial question—determining how our performance in the physical world affects our experience in the next world.

Some Traditional Theories of a Justly Devised Physical World

Of all the theological and philosophical issues that tease our minds regarding the theory of how a just God could devise a physical creation, the most tantalizing is the matter of theodicy, the "vindication of divine justice in the face of the existence of evil" (*American Heritage Dictionary*). Put succinctly, if God is good, how can there be evil in His world?

If we do not believe in God, we need not trouble ourselves by searching for justice in the physical world. We may try to impose order in society or to be fair in our relations with others if we think it worthwhile to do so. But from such a perspective we do not expect justice in creation as a whole—natural laws of cause and effect describe our changing planet and our relationship to the phenomenal world in general. This view is not necessarily dreary or fatalistic, but it must, by definition, accept the "purpose" of physical reality as being that which we invent or attribute to a system which has no inherent purpose of its own.

But when we ascribe to physical reality and our participation in it a divine foundation and rationale, we must assume that there is an ultimate purpose latent within the system and an overriding justice, a justice which pervades our physical experience and relates our daily lives to our divine origin. Consequently, it is from those who affirm a belief in a divine Creator that the most powerful statements on justice in the phenomenal world have come. Before we examine the Bahá'í theory or paradigm of the physical world, we would do well to examine some well-known attempts to deal with the question of theodicy. Such a cursory survey will serve to establish the fundamental issues at stake and several of the more notable solutions to the question.

Plato's Republic (ca. 468 B.C.)

Though one of the earliest recorded attempts to discover justice in the physical world, Plato's dialogue The Republic has endured as one of the most influential and penetrating discussions of the subject. Basing his artful dialogue on the ideas of his teacher Socrates, Plato avoids much direct discussion of theology per se, though he does attribute the infusion of spiritual qualities into physical creation as the emanation of a single divine source, the Good. According to 'Abdu'l-Bahá, the source of these monotheistic beliefs, for which Socrates was later executed, was Judaism:

> He visited the Holy Land and studied with the prophets of Israel, acquiring principles of their philosophical teaching and a knowledge of their advanced arts and sciences. After his return to Greece he founded the system known as the unity of God. (Promulgation 406)

In another passage 'Abdu'l-Bahá states that the basic evidence of the Judaic influence is found in Socrates' concept of the unity of God and in his teaching about the immortality of the soul:

> It is recorded in eastern histories that Socrates journeyed to Palestine and Syria and there, from men learned in the things of God, acquired certain spiritual truths; that when he returned to Greece, he promulgated two beliefs: one, the unity of God, and the other, the immortality of the soul after its separation from the body. . . . (Selections 55)

Bahá'u'lláh also praises the thinking and influence of Socrates, particularly his theory of "forms," sometimes called the theory of "ideas," the assertion that physical reality is but a reflection of a higher spiritual reality:

> He it is who perceived a unique, a tempered, and a pervasive nature in things, bearing the closest likeness to the human spirit, and he discovered this nature to be distinct from the substance of things in their refined form. He hath a special pronouncement on this weighty theme. (*Tablets of Bahá'u'lláh* 146)

While Bahá'u'lláh may have been alluding to any number of Plato's dialogues that discuss the theory of ideas, He probably was referring to *The Republic,* the avowed objective of which is to define justice in the broadest sense of the word. Though ostensibly an attempt to discover the nature of justice in the individual, the dialogue becomes a powerful analysis of how we can use our physical experience to learn spiritual lessons.

The work begins by examining some of the traditional views of justice. Next the character Socrates suggests that the best means of understanding justice in the individual is by first trying to determine how justice works in the larger arena of the state. He argues that if we wish to discover justice in an individual life, it would be easier to begin by defining justice in "larger proportions" (Plato 55) in order that it might be more clearly perceived. So it is that the participants in the dialogue begin devising a just republic.

The resulting discussion provides a fruitful series of analogies —the individual compared to a state and, by implication, the state compared to physical reality itself. In effect, the search for justice goes far beyond any explicit political doctrine and tackles the essential issue of how physical reality can be perceived as having spiritual significance.

After lengthy debate and consideration of what creates justice in a political structure, the participants in the dialogue conclude that the guiding principle of a just state must be propriety—each thing doing that for which it is especially suited. All of the constituent parts should then work in harmony for the mutual benefit of the whole. The rulers, the wisest and most magnanimous of the citizenry, should make the decisions; the military, the most physically able, should protect the state; the poets should concoct allegorized myths and parables to explain abstract principles to the unlearned masses; the craftsmen should make the tools; the farmers should produce the food; the shopkeepers should distribute the goods.

The careful detail with which Plato builds an aristocracy has led many to conclude that The Republic is primarily a political treatise. Plato has even been vehemently censured by some critics for the rigidity and, as they perceive it, the totalitarian implications of his political exercise.* Such readers seem to misrepresent the literal portrait of the republic, however, and they totally miss the allegorical intent of the work—defining justice in the individual.

As with the state, for example, the overriding principle of justice in the individual is the harmony produced when one abides by the rule of propriety, each constituent faculty of the individual doing that for which it is best suited, and the whole organism striving harmoniously toward one unified goal. The rational mind, like the rulers or guardians of the state, makes decisions and governs one's aspirations. The body, like the military in the state, defends the physical edifice, and so on:

> Only when he has linked these parts together in well-tempered harmony and has made himself one man instead of many, will he be ready to go about whatever he may have to do, whether it be making money and satisfying bodily wants, or business transactions, or the affairs of state. . . . Any action which tends to break down this habit will be for him unjust. . . . (Plato 142)

Injustice is the result of disharmony among our human faculties, when, for example, we allow lesser faculties to usurp the governing authority of the mind or allow ourselves to become

---

*See Karl R. Popper, ''The Spell of Plato,'' The Open Society and Its Enemies, 2 vols., 5th rev. ed. (Princeton, N.J.: Princeton Univ. Press, 1966), vol. 1.

fragmented in such a way that we are in a condition of internal warfare or turmoil. Injustice is thus a violation of internal propriety and harmony.

For Plato the logical extension of the principle of harmony and propriety is a doctrine of transcendence or progressive enlightenment. In the same way that the political state cannot remain static, neither can the individual. What keeps the state in motion toward perfection is the guidance of the whole toward the objectives which the guardians (or philosopher-kings) have perceived as a result of their enlightenment. Similarly, in the individual the mind must gain insight and then discover the best means of translating that insight into beneficial action.

To demonstrate how human spiritual progress takes place, Socrates, in Book VII of *The Republic,* uses an analogy which explains his theory of the "forms," the famous allegory of the cave. In this analogy Socrates portrays men bound in a cave and facing a wall. Behind and above them is the mouth of the cave, in front of which people pass by. A fire outside the cave causes the passing figures to cast shadows on the wall of the cave so that to the bound prisoners, who cannot turn to see the source of those shadows, the distorted images are reality. But because the philosopher-king yearns for knowledge and enlightenment, he breaks free from his bonds and turns to see the source of those images. Through further effort he scales the rough walls of the cave and peers out to see the higher reality, the figures themselves and the fire that is the source of light. Because he persists, he ventures out from the cave into the sunlight. But the brightness of the sun forces him to look at the ground and shade his eyes. There he notices the shadows of trees and other objects.

As his eyes become accustomed to the light, he is able to look up and see the objects themselves. Ultimately, he sees above and beyond all objects the sun itself, the source of all reality:

> He would need, then, to grow accustomed before he could see things in that upper world. At first it would be easiest to make out shadows, and then the images of men and things reflected in water, and later on the things themselves. After that, it would be easier to watch the heavenly bodies and the sky itself by night, looking at the

light of the moon and stars rather than the Sun and the Sun's light in
the day-time. . . .

Last of all, he would be able to look at the Sun and contemplate
its nature, not as it appears when reflected in water or any alien
medium, but as it is in itself in its own domain. (229–30)

Having attained an immensely increased level of perception about
the reality of things, and having ascertained the force animating
creation, the philosopher-king must now accomplish another difficult part of his task.

As Socrates explains, the knowledgeable one must now return
to the cave whence he came in order to assist the other prisoners to
become enlightened. But coming so suddenly from sunlight into a
world of darkness and shadow, the philosopher-king at first seems
clumsy and awkward:

Coming suddenly out of the sunlight, his eyes would be filled with
darkness. He might be required once more to deliver his opinion on
those shadows, in competition with the prisoners who had never been
released, while his eyesight was still dim and unsteady; and it might
take some time to become used to the darkness. They would laugh at
him and say that he had gone up only to come back with his sight
ruined; it was worth no one's while even to attempt the ascent. If they
could lay hands on the man who was trying to set them free and lead
them up, they would kill him. (230–31)

The allusion to the killing of the philosopher-king might be seen as
poignantly foreshadowing Socrates' own execution for his teachings, as well as the suffering and death of the Prophets of God, but
that is not Plato's primary objective here. Since the divisions of the
state are analogous to human faculties, the philosopher-king represents the combined mental and spiritual capacities or, possibly, the
soul. The journey of the prisoner from image to sunlight might thus
depict the ascent of the soul of man from attachment to the
mundane to an understanding of the divine attributes or qualities
which shadowy images can only hint at. But just as those who are
still imprisoned reject the enlightened guidance of the returning
philosopher-king, so our appetitive nature resists the dictates of the

spirit. It is only with great willpower and persistent effort that we can relinquish our attachment to earthly concerns.

While the cave analogy may have various applications, for Plato the principal value of the parable is in dramatizing how physical creation reflects the abstract "forms" or "ideas" of the spiritual plane of existence. It is in this sense that Plato has designated the just or proper function of physical reality to be its ability to give metaphoric or symbolic form to metaphysical concepts, what are called in the Bahá'í writings "divine attributes," "spiritual qualities," or "names of God." Plato further hints at the nature of his monotheistic beliefs when he describes how all these attributes or "forms" are but emanations of one primary source, the Good. In his analogy Socrates compares the Good to the sun, since the Good illuminates or makes understandable all other realities. In his introductory notes to chapter 23 of Book VI the translator Francis Macdonald Cornford attempts to clarify Plato's notion of the Good:

> In Greek "the Good" is normally synonymous with "Goodness itself." This is the supreme Form or Essence manifested not only in the special kinds of moral goodness, Justice, Courage, etc., but throughout all Nature (for every living creature has its own "good") and especially in the beautiful and harmonious order of the heavenly bodies. . . . The knowledge of the Good, on which well-being depends, is now to include an understanding of the moral and physical order of the whole universe. As the object of a purpose attributed to a divine Reason operating in the world, this supreme Good makes the world intelligible, as a work of human craftsmanship becomes intelligible when we see the purpose it is designed to serve. (Cornford, in Plato 212).

Socrates continues in the cave analogy to amplify the process by which the proximity to or vision of the Good empowers the guardian to return to the cave and lead the other prisoners out of bondage. That is, after the guardian gains his insight, he must return to the world of images, the mundane world of cave and shadow. In terms of the individual, the return to the world of images might allude to the transformation of character as our daily habits become sanctified through divine guidance.

According to Plato in his dramatization of Socratic thought, the justification of temporal reality thus lies in the very fabric of creation itself. The physical world is a divinely ordained teaching device through which man can ascend from the depths of blindness to the heights of enlightenment by learning to discern the spiritual attributes reflected in the phenomenal world. There is, therefore, no sense of disdain for physical reality, but there is a gradual relinquishing of the need for physical analogues as one learns spiritual lessons. So-called Platonic love, for example, is not so much a disregard for physical love as it is a process by which one ascends from physical attraction and sexual expression of love to a recognition and appreciation of the spiritual attributes in the beloved. This transformation of love occurs when one realizes that such attributes are, in fact, the source of the physical attraction itself.* From here one can proceed to a love of the spiritual attributes in all mankind and ultimately to a love of creation as a whole.

From the Platonic point of view, evil or injustice in the phenomenal world, at least injustice as it is perpetrated by mankind, results from ignorance. Plato argues that no one does evil in full knowledge because to do evil or injustice is, ultimately, to injure one's own soul, and no one would willingly inflict misery on himself. Any learning which ignores the spiritual purpose of man may consequently bring about more harm than good by bestowing power without the wisdom of how to use that power for beneficial purposes.

Plato's examination of justice both in the individual and, by inference, in the physical world as a whole has had a remarkable impact on the history of Western thought with regard to the concept of how physical reality can be an appropriate environment for essentially spiritual beings. Whether in the works of Saint Augustine or in the philosophy of the romantic poets, the scope of Plato's influence is still being felt. And yet, for all its merit, Plato's attempt

---

*The process of ascent from physical attraction to an appreciation of spiritual attributes Plato sets forth explicitly in the dialogue *Symposium*.

at theodicy does not deal forcefully with such matters as the relationship between the Creator and the creation or how the seemingly arbitrary accidents and disasters of physical life function in accord with divine justice.

The Book of Job (500–300 B.C.)

Composed sometime between 500 and 300 B.C. (Gordis 218), the Book of Job examines justice in the physical world from the point of view of an explicitly monotheistic belief. To a certain extent the work takes up where Plato leaves off. Here God is not simply the sum total of virtue—Plato's "Good"; He is cognitive, aware of each individual life, concerned for His creation. If we put aside the numerous disputes over composition and textual integrity, we can see in this masterpiece of world literature some issues of justice not raised in Plato's dialogue—how to maintain a belief in a just God in spite of the appearance in the physical world of arbitrary injustice.

A didactic poem of dialogue "imbedded in a prose tale" (Gordis 9), the Book of Job revolves around a man who has long remained the emblem of human patience and humility in the face of untold suffering and apparent injustice. The story begins with Job as a prosperous and respected chieftain. When Satan contends that Job's exemplary fidelity is the result of Job's prosperity in life, God gives Satan permission to test Job, and God wagers that Job will prove his worth.

After a series of disasters that deprive Job of his possessions and most of his family, he is grief stricken, but he still praises God. Not satisfied, Satan proposes that Job suffer injury to his person. Hence God gives Satan permission to inflict on Job a loathsome disease. Job's wife tempts him to despair and to curse God, and three friends who have ostensibly come to comfort Job accuse him of suffering the consequences of irreligion and iniquity. Convinced of his own innocence, Job rejects their accusations, but in his mounting anguish he pleads with God to speak to him directly.

Eventually, God does speak to Job as a voice from a whirlwind and in lengthy, powerful speeches enumerates examples of His awesome authority and power. He then asks rhetorically if Job has the capacity to control the forces of the universe or understand the complexity of the laws governing the stars, the animals, or the weather. Job readily confesses his own weakness. After a further vision of God's might, Job submits, attests to God's majesty, and is restored. In an epilogue God condemns the three friends, gives Job twice what he had before, returns his family, and gives him twice the normal life span.

In the New Testament James praises Job as an example of steadfastness (James 5:11), as does Muḥammad in the Qur'án (38:40–44) and 'Abdu'l-Bahá in *Paris Talks:* "Job proved the fidelity of his love for God by being faithful through his great adversity, as well as during the prosperity of his life" (50). But at the crux of the story, for our purposes, are Job's response to injustice and the story's ending.

Of course, the portrait of God literally debating with Satan is generally accepted as mythological tradition, in the same way that we accept the story of Adam and Eve as symbolism or allegory, not as literal history. Thus when the tests come upon Job, they come from Satan. But just as the Bahá'í writings interpret scriptural allusions to Satan as giving in to one's baser instincts as opposed to turning to God, possibly the author of Job has intended a similar meaning. Therefore, the tests of Satan may represent Job's inner temptation to rebel against faith and belief.

Job's response to Satan's testing is human but noble: He never denies his faith or despairs of ultimate redemption. Most important, he does not accede to his friends' assertion that the torment is somehow deserved. For example, his companion Eliphaz responds to Job's lamentation by implying that no one ever suffers unjustly:

> "Think now, who that was innocent ever perished?
>   Or where were the upright cut off?
> As I have seen, those who plow iniquity
>   and sow trouble reap the same." (Job 4:7–8)

Job answers that he has "not denied the words of the Holy One" (6:10) and further challenges his friend's rebuke:

"He who withholds kindness from a friend
    forsakes the fear of the Almighty.
My brethren are treacherous as a torrent-bed,
    as freshets that pass away,
which are dark with ice,
    and where the snow hides itself.
In time of heat they disappear;
    when it is hot, they vanish from their place." (6:14–17)

Extending this metaphor to portray further his friends' lack of steadfastness, Job characterizes his companions as fearful of sharing in his fate: "You see my calamity, and are afraid" (6:21). "Teach me," he continues, "and I will be silent; make me understand how I have erred" (6:24).

Job knows that the reasons for his afflictions, whatever they may be, have nothing to do with God's retribution for his behavior. He is confident of his own goodness. He is human and feels his pain, but he never denies his faith in God. For this he is rewarded with more than he had before:

> And the Lord restored the fortunes of Job, when he had prayed for his friends; and the Lord gave Job twice as much as he had before. . . . And the Lord blessed the latter days of Job more than his beginning. . . . (42:10, 12)

But while Job prospers in the end, we are left with a theological enigma, to say the least. True, Job becomes the emblem of fidelity and steadfastness, but in what sense has a vision of a just God or a just physical reality been revealed?

The implicit justification contained in the closing poetic speeches by God seems to imply a power beyond the ken of men, but there is no attempt to affirm that the voice out of the whirlwind has tested Job with some purpose in mind. For the author of the closing prose epilogue (who may or may not be the author of the poetic sections), justice lies in the physical redemption of Job. He gets paid off, as it were. And yet the payoff hardly reveals a logic or justice in the testing itself, something that has caused scholars and theologians alike to speculate endlessly.

While it is not the purpose here to untangle the web of theological paradox, we can discover several themes that unify the work and give important insight into the efforts of human beings to perceive the presence of justice in physical reality. First, as an exemplum, or narrative that conveys a moral, the story of Job works well to demonstrate that justice is eventually done in God's world. Of course, in the story justice seems to be accomplished on the physical plane of existence—but is it? The story is a poem, after all, replete with symbolism and imagery. Just as the initial debate between God and Satan is symbolic, so the rest of the story may be as well. The final restoration of Job's riches may be symbolic of a celestial reunion, an otherworldly rectifying and justifying of Job's exemplary patience in this life.

Second, the story focuses not on justifying God's ways to man but on proclaiming forcefully that even the righteous are tested in this life, which is how 'Abdu'l-Bahá explains the meaning of Job's life:

> What trials, calamities and perplexities did he not endure! But these tests were like unto the fire and his holiness Job was like unto pure gold. Assuredly gold is purified by being submitted to the fire and if it contain any alloy or imperfection, it will disappear. That is the reason why violent tests become the cause of the everlasting glory of the righteous and are conducive to the destruction and disappearance of the unrighteous. (*Tablets of Abdul-Baha Abbas* 3:655)

From 'Abdu'l-Bahá's perspective the poem is a depiction of spiritual growth. It begins with a man of position and prosperity, a good man, but a man with as yet untried potential. As Job's tests increase in severity, he ultimately gives way to despair, though he never relinquishes his faith. In the end he is rewarded not with some final or complete insight into God's actions but with a vision of God's grandeur, something quite beyond the simplistic understanding of righteousness and justice exhibited earlier by Job's friends, and something more emotionally powerful and complete than Plato's allusions to the Good.

After the voice describes in poetic eloquence the loftiness of the Creator, the awed Job responds meekly:

"I had heard of thee by the hearing of the ear,
    but now my eye sees thee;
therefore I despise myself,
    and repent in dust and ashes." (Job 42:5–6)

Foreshadowing Isaiah's prophecy (Isa. 6:9–10) repeated by Christ (Matt. 13:14–16) regarding the danger of believers relying on others for their knowledge of the truth rather than on investigating beliefs for themselves, Job has concluded with a definition of justice from his own point of view. For Job a just state within the individual is experiencing the reality of God; such a knowledge of God enables Job to withstand the contrary opinions of others and the adverse personal circumstances he encounters in the physical world.

According to Old Testament scholar Selton Pollock the justice portrayed in the poem is thus not a cosmological vision but a purely personal one, a profound transition in the character of Job. Instead of acting solely out of fear of God, Job comes to act out of a love of God's beauty:

> The progress of Job's faith can be plainly traced through the story. It is evident that his original piety had been largely influenced by motives of fear. . . . And when tragedy breaks in upon him, we discover the main source of his moral earnestness, for he exclaims: "This is what I feared—and now it has come to pass" (3:25). (Pollock 270)

After Job's passage through the fire of tests, he no longer operates mechanically. His understanding, and therefore his faith as well, are firmly grounded in the lessons he has learned from his tests. He may not have a complete vision of God's plan for mankind, but he does realize profoundly that the suffering he has endured has resulted in his own spiritual development.

Boethius' Consolation of Philosophy (ca. 522 A.D.)

About a thousand years after the composition of Job, Anicius Boethius (480–524) wrote *The Consolation of Philosophy*, a work which takes an approach wholly different from Plato's and Job's treatments of justice in the physical world. Though affirming the providential hand of God at work in human history, Boethius advocates the abandonment of concern for physical reality as the sanest and most just response to this life.

His examination of justice was composed under the most pragmatic of circumstances. A fifth-century Italian scholar and consul to Theodoric the Ostrogoth, Boethius was a victim of political machinations for which he was imprisoned and condemned to death. While awaiting execution, he composed *The Consolation of Philosophy* as a dialogue between the persona Boethius and the allegorical figure Dame Philosophy. In the course of the conversation Dame Philosophy attempts to teach the distraught Boethius about God's justice, primarily in relation to an individual's life. Her responses to Boethius' tirades against the blatant injustice of the physical world form the basis of a Christian stoicism that had a tremendous influence on medieval Christianity.

At the beginning of the work Boethius asks the obvious question: If God is, whence cometh evil? Like Job, he is beset with unjust tribulation, but beyond his own circumstances he is concerned with the way in which the world itself seems prey to the iniquity of unjust men. Therefore, after explaining his own unjust imprisonment as an example of evil, he catalogs an array of injustices in the phenomenal world:

> I see honest men lying crushed with the fear which smites them after the result of my perilous case: wicked men one and all encouraged to dare every crime without fear of punishment, nay, with hope of rewards for the accomplishment thereof: the innocent I see robbed not merely of their peace and safety, but even of all chance of defending themselves. (14)

Dame Philosophy tells Boethius that his problem results from his having "forgotten what you are":

> Now therefore I have found out to the full the manner of your sickness, and how to attempt the restoring of your health. You are overwhelmed

> by this forgetfulness of yourself: hence you have been thus sorrowing
> that you are exiled and robbed of all your possessions. You do not
> know the aim and end of all things; hence you think that if men are
> worthless and wicked, they are powerful and fortunate. You have
> forgotten by what methods the universe is guided. . . . (18)

She then proceeds to prove to Boethius that his grief is unwarrant-
ed. First, she shows Boethius that he has had good fortune as well
as bad. Next, she reminds him of the vanity of worldly desires. The
very treasures that are universally prized—riches, positions, king-
doms, earthly glory, fame, nobility of birth, lusts of the flesh—are
all actually harmful and not to be desired. She then discusses the
source of true happiness: a belief in and understanding of God
Himself.

She quickly proves to Boethius that, inasmuch as God is
absolutely good, He can do no evil. What Boethius perceives as
evil is either not of God or else not properly understood. In the
course of further discussion Dame Philosophy distinguishes between Fate and Providence. Fate, she notes, is seemingly fickle; no
one knows what his or her situation will be tomorrow. But Fate is
ultimately subject to Providence, which is derived from God's
eternal plan:

> Thus is the world governed for the best if a directness, which rests in
> the intelligence of God, puts forth an order of causes which may not
> swerve. This order restrains by its own unchangeableness changeable
> things, which might otherwise run hither and thither at random.
> Wherefore in disposing the universe this limitation directs all for good,
> though to you who are not strong enough to comprehend the whole
> order, all seems confusion and disorder. (93)

Dame Philosophy's concept of man's limited perception of divine
order lies at the heart of the Boethian consolation. It implies a
stoicism both in regard to historical events, whose final implications we cannot fathom, and in regard to our own individual lives,
which ultimately find justice only in the next world.

Boethius' primary concern is focused on the individual, and his work contends that so long as the virtuous man pursues the Highest Good, anything which befalls him will, in the long run, be utilized to assist in his ultimate fulfillment; in short, justice will be done: "The fortune of those who are in possession of virtue, or are gaining it, or advancing therein, is entirely good, whatever it be, while for those who remain in wickedness, their fortune is the worst" (99).

The concluding argument for justice in God's creation is explained by Dame Philosophy in the fifth and final book, where she avers that there is no such thing as chance; everything occurs with purpose and under God's jurisdiction. Dame Philosophy also confirms the simultaneous functioning of free will and foreknowledge: God's foreknowledge of events has no causal effect on our free decisions.

There is no substantial discussion about the relationship between our freely chosen course of action and our experience in the afterlife. Boethius simply affirms that justice will be done and that we should, therefore, be detached from the trials of this earthly life. The work does not attempt to explain why God does not intervene in history to assist His creation except to imply that justice will eventually be done on earth as it is in the spiritual realm.

The Consolation of Philosophy thus responds primarily to the plight of the individual and focuses on evil or injustice perpetrated by malefactors. Boethius asserts the providence and benignancy of God and affirms that in this life virtue—the pursuit of the good—is the individual's goal, the attainment of which brings its own rewards as well as the promise of justice in the hereafter. Hence the appropriate response to injustice in this life is a stoical attitude, a philosophical position that upholds *contemptu mundi* (disdain for the world), the watchword of medieval Christianity, just as the Wheel of Fortune became a key metaphor for Boethian Christianity.* Even though stoicism implies a condemnation of God's creation, Boethian philosophy views earthly ascendancy as ephem-

---

*The Latin phrase meaning "disdain for the world" was the title of a treatise, *De Contemptu Mundi,* by Pope Innocent III. It was commonly used to convey the attitude of most medieval Church authorities that the proper activity in this life is to reject temporal pursuits and prepare for the afterlife.

eral, capricious, arbitrary. The just and wise course of action for humankind is to disdain involvement in the physical world and concentrate on preparing for the next world.

Boethius' work is by no means unique in its response to the question of justice in God's creation, but it was a seminal work that helped console people in the Middle Ages who daily confronted all manner of apparent injustice, including illiteracy, social and economic oppression, an extremely high rate of child mortality, and plagues that eradicated up to 60 percent of the populace in some areas. In such an atmosphere asceticism and the monastic ideal which Boethius' philosophy was used to uphold seemed sane responses to physical reality.

Milton's Paradise Lost (1667 A.D.)

More than a thousand years after Boethius, the English poet John Milton wrote *Paradise Lost* as an attempt to explain justice in the physical world in terms of the intervention of God through the sacrifice of His Son. In the course of this magnificent poem, Milton delineates a relatively complete paradigm of physical creation which affirms the necessity of good works coupled with knowledge and free will, together with the guidance and assistance of God. In this sense, Milton confirms the value of participation in the world described by Plato, vindicates the majesty of God alluded to in Job, and spells out the historical perspective which Boethius asserts but fails to explain.

Contemplating the most worthy theme to which he could devote his epical talents, Milton rejected his initial idea of writing an account of the Arthurian legend and determined instead to "assert Eternal Providence, / And justify the ways of God to men" (*Paradise Lost* 1.25–26). To bring his theology and philosophy to life in *Paradise Lost* Milton employed the Edenic myth to portray God's justice. So confident was he that he could present justice from God's point of view (thereby eclipsing what Boethius had done) that he dared to include God as a major character in the work.

To a certain extent Milton in *Paradise Lost* was dealing with the same problem that is at the heart of Boethius' work—how to account for injustice and evil in a world wrought by an omnipotent and beneficent Deity. But Milton was predominantly concerned with the historical perspective (the very thing Boethius avoided), even though his treatment of the fall of Satan from heaven and of Adam and Eve from Edenic grace offers sound and dramatic examples of free will in motion.

As a literal portrayal of history the work fails; but it is clear that Milton had no such intention for his magnum opus—he certainly did not presume to know what God thought at a given moment, nor was he theologically such a literalist. Nevertheless, the theology and philosophy we can elicit from the work are, by and large, logically consistent and theologically satisfying.

Milton responds to the problem of the origin of evil with a doctrine of free will regarding both the inception of sin in the mind of Lucifer and the negligence of Adam and Eve when they fail to follow the clear dictates of God's law. Milton answers the question of God's providence and ascendancy by showing how man will be redeemed in spite of himself and how evil machinations will ultimately serve only to bring about a greater good.

Milton treats the origin of evil in the story of Satan's rebellion against God, an embellishment of the biblical myth wherein Lucifer begets sin by contemplating through his pride an unholy revolt in heaven. But Satan rebels not because he is incapable of understanding the justice in worshiping God and the Son (Christ before His incarnation) but because he *will* not. Satan later reveals that he is aware of the vanity in rebelling against an omnipotent force. But he persists in rejecting the just authority of God.

In one soliloquy the fallen Satan indicates that he misses what he had in heaven, that he knows God's laws are just and proper, and that his rebellion was wrong and undeserved. He knows that God is ever-forgiving and would receive him back should he repent, but Satan will not. On the border of God's new creation, intent on further mischief, he is reminded of what he once had "Till pride and worse ambition threw me down/Warring in heav'n against heav'n's matchless King" (4.40–41). At this crucial juncture Satan acknowledges forthrightly God's ascendancy and justice:

> He deserved no such return
> From me, whom he created what I was
> In that bright eminence, and with his good
> Upbraided none; nor was his service hard.
> What could be less than to afford him praise,
> The easiest recompense, and pay him thanks,
> How due! (4.42–48)

Yet in a magnificent study of willful evil, Satan continues his malicious design, knowing he can never overcome God but hoping at least to make Adam and Eve as miserable as he and to force God to reject His own creation. Of course, the only way for Satan to redeem himself is through submission, and that is the key to his dilemma. In his pride he cannot submit, will not, even when he knows that it is just, proper, and pragmatically beneficial for him to do so:

> Nay cursed be thou, since against his thy will
> Chose freely what it now so justly rues.
>
> . . . .
>
> O then at last relent: is there no place
> Left for repentance, none for pardon left?
> None left but by submission; and that word
> Disdain forbids me, and my dread of shame
> Among the Spirits beneath, whom I seduced
> With other promises and other vaunts
> Than to submit, boasting I could subdue
> Th' Omnipotent. (4.71–72, 79–86)

To understand the dramatic importance of this passage, we must pay careful attention to the very real possibility of Satan's redemption. According to Milton's theological beliefs, redemption is available to Satan, but he consciously decides to reject it.

In addition to the doctrine of God's forgiveness as part of a system of divine justice, and closely related to it, is Milton's portrayal of the simultaneous existence of God's foreknowledge and omnipotence with man's free will. But instead of simply affirming this belief, Milton has the character of God Himself explain why He has allowed Satan to rebel and evil to intrude in His creation. In a dialogue with His Son, God states that if beings were forced to recognize His authority and beneficence, they could not be said to understand His nature, nor would such obedience be praiseworthy or significant:

> Freely they stood who stood, and fell who fell.
> Not free, what proof could they have giv'n sincere
> Of true allegiance, constant faith or love,
> Where only what they needs must do, appeared,
> Not what they would? What praise could they receive?
> What pleasure I from such obedience paid,
> When will and reason (reason also is choice)
> Useless and vain, of freedom both despoiled. . . .   (3.102–09)

God goes on to state that though He foreknew the angels would rebel, just as He knows that man will fail in Eden, He does not cause these events to occur:

> they themselves decreed
> Their own revolt, not I. If I foreknew,
> Foreknowledge had no influence on their fault,
> Which had no less proved certain unforeknown.   (3.116–19)

But it is in the remaining books of the epic that Milton approaches his primary justification of God's ways to man. After Satan succeeds in seducing Eve and Adam, they confess their guilt and repent. Their punishment is banishment from Eden, and their departure is the end of the plot per se, but it is by no means the end of the epic. In preparation for their new life God sends the angel Michael to comfort Adam and Eve by explaining to them the ultimate triumph of God's plan. In the last two books of the poem the couple is shown a vision that constitutes both a history lesson and a finishing touch for Milton's theology. Man will become degenerate through sin until God, out of His mercy, sends his Son. Through the Son's sacrifice, man will be redeemed to a position higher than that which he occupied before the Fall.

Michael's vision of *felix lapsus* (fortunate fall) so excites Adam that he exclaims:

"O goodness infinite, goodness immense!
That all this good of evil shall produce,
And evil turn to good; more wonderful
Than that which by creation first brought forth
Light out of darkness!" (12.469–73)

But Michael is quick to caution Adam and Eve that their knowledge of the fortuitous and just outcome of history is not sufficient for their own personal salvation. They must add deeds, faith, and other virtues to this "right reason" (12.84).* If they do, their ultimate condition will be happier than the Edenic bliss they have lost through willful neglect:

only add
Deeds to thy knowledge answerable, add faith,
Add virtue, patience, temperance, add love,
By name to come called charity, the soul
Of all the rest: then wilt thou not be loth
To leave this Paradise, but shalt possess
A paradise within thee, happier far. (12.581–87)

The conclusion of Milton's presentation of God's actions, therefore, is a clearer and more complete justification of the nature of physical reality than the previous works we have examined. Unlike the God of Job, Whose justice we must guess at, and beyond Boethius' blind faith that justice in any significant way is veiled from man's eyes or else reserved for the afterlife, Milton's God does explain the divine rationale for the creation itself and for His

---

*"Right reason," as Milton uses it in Michael's discussion about reason as the guiding faculty in spiritual growth, is defined by Douglas Bush in *The Complete Poetical Works of John Milton* as "the philosophic conscience, the power, implanted by God in all men, to apprehend truth and moral law (a Christian legacy from classical thought)" (566).

relationship to mankind. Instead of simply asserting God's historical ascendancy, Milton delineates it through a historical recounting. But, most important, Milton's God is not mechanistic, not impersonal. Like a loving but wise parent, He watches His creation, knows mankind will fail, but, in order to test and teach, withholds intervention. Ultimately God will intervene, Milton explains, and guide the course of history toward its benign objectives. Even those events which presently seem destructive—the rebellion of Satan, the fall of mankind, the iniquity of the wayward—God will eventually employ to achieve propitious results.

The attempts by Plato, Job, Boethius, and Milton to understand and vindicate humanity's proper relationship to the physical world are partially successful. Incrementally, each seems to reflect a gradually more encompassing understanding of the divine purposes latent within physical reality. Moreover, the combined responses of these works seem to offer important and largely successful answers to the question of theodicy. Certainly the value of these works to the Bahá'í is reflected in the degree to which the Bahá'í writings substantiate and clarify the points we have seen discussed. However, one crucial question remains unanswered—why God would allow human history to proceed for so long before He would intervene. A corollary of this question points to the larger issue —why would a loving God intervene only once? A brief examination of the Bahá'í writings shows the extent to which the Bahá'í beliefs correspond to these attempts at theodicy. More significantly, after reviewing the Bahá'í response, we can lay the foundation for the task of discovering the entire paradigm of physical reality as it is revealed throughout the Bahá'í writings.

A Bahá'í Response to Plato

The essence of Plato's explanation of the basis for justice in the physical world consists of two general observations. First, Plato expresses the belief that physical reality corresponds to and is a reflection of spiritual reality. To Plato this correspondence is no accident, no incidental quality of physical creation, but, rather, is the essential nature and purpose of all created things. Second, Plato posits the theory that man can, by relying on his higher self, discern the spiritual messages that physical creation has to impart. These messages consist of the spiritual qualities, the abstract virtues or attributes, which exist in some ethereal state in the spiritual realm but which are presented to man in concrete form so that they can be initially perceived and acquired.

According to Plato, the twofold arrangement is the basis for justice in the physical world. Human justice itself is the proprietorial harmony or integrity of our faculties wherein each capacity functions as it is ordained to, with the mind subordinating the lesser capacities in a coordinated ascent.

Plato's view of spiritual education is remarkably parallel to the Bahá'í concept of the divine purpose of physical creation. Bahá'u'lláh states that "every created thing is a sign of the revelation of God" (*Gleanings* 184) and that every human being has the capacity to recognize this relationship:

> He hath endowed every soul with the capacity to recognize the signs of God. How could He, otherwise, have fulfilled His testimony unto men, if ye be of them that ponder His Cause in their hearts. He will never deal unjustly with any one, neither will He task a soul beyond its power. (*Gleanings* 105–06)

And yet, as rewarding and influential as Plato's work has been, it is not complete. One missing ingredient, for example, is the idea of a Divine Being, a Creator Who assists His creation at every turn. For while Plato's concept of the Good hints at his monotheistic belief, Plato never really attributes to this entity any cognitive powers. The Good is the amalgamation and epitome of all virtue. Therefore, while the ascent from the cave of ignorance to the light of knowledge is due to the emanations from the Good, this mystic source does not in Plato's description exert any conscious effort to bring about the philosopher-king's transformation, nor does it lend any overt aid to the ascent of humankind. The journey from darkness to light seems to be the result of individual insight and determination on the part of the philosopher-king.

Plato did not intend his work to be a study of the Deity, but his model of human transformation is still at variance with the Bahá'í concept of a God Who is aware of, concerned with, and actively intervening to assist His creation.

Even if we interpret Plato's specialized individuals, the philosopher-kings, as metaphorical representations of the Prophets, the analogy fails to account for the repeated statements by the Manifestations that they do nothing on their own authority (see John 14:10) but speak and act as God directs them. Bahá'u'lláh explained the source of His knowledge when He wrote:

> This thing is not from Me, but from One Who is Almighty and All-Knowing. And He bade Me lift up My voice between earth and heaven, and for this there befell Me what hath caused the tears of every man of understanding to flow. (*Proclamation* 57)

> By My Life! Not of Mine own volition have I revealed Myself, but God, of His own choosing, hath manifested Me. (qtd. in Shoghi Effendi, *God Passes By* 102)

The dedication of the Manifestations to the instruction of man, even at the cost of their own lives, might parallel the suffering and rejection which the philosopher-king experiences when he descends into the cave to lead others toward a higher reality. But Plato's avowed purpose, as we have already observed, is to construct an analogy for justice in the individual, not to portray the process of divine revelation; and insofar as *The Republic* justifies how a physical experience can provide a spiritual understanding, Plato's work is a milestone in human thought.

A Bahá'í Response to Job

With the Book of Job we go beyond the sense of Plato s Good to consider a Being Who is independent and cognitive. What we do not get from Job is an understanding or appreciation of God's plan for humankind. As Old Testament scholar Robert Gordis notes in his study of Job, we must look elsewhere in the Bible for that:

> Moreover, when God finally appears out of the whirlwind He does *not* assure Job of His protection and love for His suffering creature. For that

theme we must look elsewhere in biblical and extra-biblical literature. Here it is the divine transcendence, the majesty and mystery of God, far removed from man and his concerns, that finds expression. (14–15)

To a certain extent, the ending of the Book of Job might seem to contradict Gordis' observation. Job's courageous response to his trials is rewarded with divine bestowals—whether they be terrestrial or otherworldly. Nevertheless, Gordis' point is essentially correct; the vision of God which the work reveals is of a being that is aware, concerned, and fully in control but at the same time mysterious and beyond any final or complete comprehension. God may have valid reasons for allowing us to be tested, but they may not always be clear to us.

The Bahá'í writings stress the logic and justice in God's actions, but we can find in various passages similar evidence of a Deity Who is beyond any complete or final understanding:

> from everlasting God hath been invested with the independent sovereignty of His exalted Being, and unto everlasting He will remain inaccessible in the transcendent majesty of His holy Essence. (The Báb 125)

Yet from other passages it is clear that it is the "holy Essence" of God which is inaccessible to the comprehension of man, not His qualities, assistance, or *modus operandi:*

> He hath extended assistance to every wayfarer, hath graciously responded to every petitioner and granted admittance to every seeker after truth. (Bahá'u'lláh, *Tablets of Bahá'u'lláh* 255)

> Then know thou that, verily, the hosts of confirmation from the Kingdom of God will assist every soul who is severed from aught else save God, is associated with the commemoration of God and is rejoiced at the glad-tidings of God. ('Abdu'l-Bahá, *Tablets of Abdul-Baha Abbas* 1:75)

Job is a poem unified around the theme of patience and faith in the midst of tribulation; it is not an attempt to compass the entire theology of its author. However, we leave Job without any satisfying appreciation of God's justice in our lives or in the evolution of man on the planet. We come away with insight into how suffering can induce growth, even in those who are basically upright; and like Job we may be awed by the majesty of God's power. But we are left to accept divine justice in general as a mystery. It is, we infer, appropriate that we be tested so that we may progress. But there is no sense in the Book of Job of a rational or systematic approach to physical reality.

A Bahá'í Response to Boethius

Boethius' vision of God and of God's justice in physical life is not that different from what we find in Job; one suffers but endures and awaits the end of suffering with noble resolve. In fact, Boethius implies a God Who is even more aloof from justice in the individual physical life than is the God of Job. The God implicit in *The Consolation of Philosophy* seems too concerned with long-range plans to be caught up in the physical difficulties of individuals because, according to Boethius, everything is justified in the afterlife. From this point of view physical reality has a value in that it informs us through our experience that all in this life is capricious, subject to change, transitory, unworthy of our attention or desire.

One major symbol of physical reality for the Christian stoic was the image of the Wheel of Fortune. Each of us is set upon a wheel that spins and stops without logic or plan. When it stops, some of us are on top and some are on the bottom, but nothing in this life is secure. Consequently, nothing material is worth pursuing. This sense of insecurity, then, was the basis for the debate in medieval Christianity about whether it was best to retire from the physical world and devote one's life to prayer and meditation (the *vita contemplativa*) or to work in the world by assisting mankind (the *vita activa*).

The Boethian philosophy does not imply that justice is nonexistent in the physical world, but Boethius does portray it as remote from individual lives. Therefore, from Boethius' perspective the just or appropriate response to physical reality is to focus attention on the next life by preparing spiritually to enter that existence. Physical activity not only seems lacking in any inherent spiritual value; it may also be a deterrent to the just purposes of humankind. Boethius thus concludes that one should be as detached as possible from the things of the physical world.

Whether Boethius intended it so or not, the Boethian philosophy became a bulwark for the contemplative life and the ascetic ideal and the manifesto of a Christian stoicism, which affirmed that it is best simply to endure life until death ends the drudgery and pain that is man's lot in the physical world. As the character Egeus says to his bereaved son Theseus in Chaucer's "Knight's Tale," a work thoroughly Boethian in philosophy, "This world nys but a thurghfare ful of wo, / And we been pilgrymes, passynge to and fro. / Deeth is an ende of every worldly soore (*Complete Poetry and Prose* 53: I, 2847–49)." (This world is but a thoroughfare full of woe, / And we are pilgrims, passing to and fro. / Death is an end of every worldly sorrow.)

Taken out of context, some passages from the Bahá'í writings might seem to indicate an attitude closely aligned with the tone of Egeus' utterance:

> Busy not thyself with this world, for with fire We test the gold, and with gold We test Our servants. (Bahá'u'lláh, *Hidden Words* 16)

> Abandon not the everlasting beauty for a beauty that must die, and set not your affections on this mortal world of dust. (Bahá'u'lláh, *Hidden Words* 26)

> Free thyself from the fetters of this world, and loose thy soul from the prison of self. Seize thy chance, for it will come to thee no more. (Bahá'u'lláh, *Hidden Words* 36)

Likewise, in another often cited passage Bahá'u'lláh indicates that, as Boethius' work implies, we may have to await the next life before we receive justice and recompense:

> Sorrow not if, in these days and on this earthly plane, things contrary to your wishes have been ordained and manifested by God, for days of

blissful joy, of heavenly delight, are assuredly in store for you. (*Gleanings* 329)

But the passage does not stop here. It goes on to hint at a vast difference between the Bahá'í view and Boethius' implications about what should be our response to physical life:

Worlds, holy and spiritually glorious, will be unveiled to your eyes. You are destined by Him, in this world and hereafter, to partake of their benefits, to share in their joys, and to obtain a portion of their sustaining grace. (*Gleanings* 329)

Thus spiritual endeavors bring rewards in this life as well as in the next life. Furthermore, the Bahá'í writings make it clear that to reject earthly life is to neglect the divine purposes for which the physical experience was created and ordained. Therefore, withdrawal from the world is viewed as inappropriate, unjust, a dereliction of divinely ordained duty and capacity.

The Bahá'í writings do caution about the dangers of the physical world, but we are commanded to participate in and to express our spiritual insights through physical activity. In fact, Bahá'u'lláh forbids mendicancy and monasticism and commands the monks and priests to abandon the solitary life in order to aid mankind:

The pious deeds of the monks and priests among the followers of the Spirit [Jesus]—upon Him be the peace of God—are remembered in His presence. In this Day, however, let them give up the life of seclusion and direct their steps towards the open world and busy themselves with that which will profit themselves and others. (*Tablets of Bahá'u'lláh* 24)

Seclude not yourselves in your churches and cloisters. Come ye out of them by My leave, and busy, then, yourselves with what will profit you and others. (*Epistle* 49)

The emphasis in the Bahá'í writings on the inextricable relationship between belief and action is so important that it is well

worth further consideration because it clearly distinguishes the
Bahá'í view of the just purposes of physical reality not only from the
views of Boethius but also from the concept of salvation through
grace as it is enunciated by what is termed the "fundamentalist"
approach to Christianity, though in reality the issue is as old as
Christianity itself and was a pivotal issue in Luther's departure from
the Roman Church to initiate the Reformation.

The fundamentalist point of view is certainly not typical of all
Christian theology. In fact, the early division in Christianity over
the issue of salvation through grace, especially as it relates to the
question of whether Christ was God, establishes for all time the
perception of many adherents of Christianity that Christ's martyrdom was the singular significant event in religious history and that
the Christian religion is, therefore, a unique expression of God's
grace, not part of an ongoing process of divine revelation. So
common a reference as the *Encyclopædia Britannica* notes this
early division among the Apostles and other followers of Christianity. It also mentions that Paul stressed a complete break with the
Judaic emphasis on law and viewed the crucifixion as "the supreme
redemptive act and also as the means of expiation for the sin of
man" (Chadwick 535). The Apostle James, the brother of Jesus,
however, viewed Christ's ministry as fulfilling the Judaic religion.
According to the *Encyclopædia Britannica:*

> Paul linked this doctrine [of salvation through the grace of God] with
> his theme that the Gospel represents liberation from the Mosaic Law.
> The latter thesis created difficulties at Jerusalem, where the church was
> under the presidency of James, the brother of Jesus. . . . the canonical
> letter ascribed to James opposes the antinomian (antilaw) interpreta-
> tions of the doctrine of justification by faith. A middle position seems
> to have been occupied by Peter. (Chadwick 535)

Christ Himself states that He did not "come to abolish the law
and the prophets; I have come not to abolish them but to fulfil
them" (Matt. 5:17). He goes on to advise his followers that their
own actions are essential to their salvation: "For I tell you, unless
your righteousness exceeds that of the scribes and Pharisees, you
will never enter the kingdom of heaven" (Matt. 5:20). He then

proceeds to reveal a fairly exacting code of law in which He abrogates some of the Judaic laws and adds others throughout the twenty-seven remaining verses of chapter 5 and the sixty-two verses of chapters 6 and 7. He ends with a stern admonition:

> And every one who hears these words of mine and does not do them will be like a foolish man who built his house upon the sand; and the rain fell, and the floods came, and the winds blew and beat against that house, and it fell; and great was the fall of it. (Matt. 7:26–27)

Paul's numerous statements deemphasizing and even denouncing works and obedience to law as having any relevance to salvation seem totally at odds with Christ's advice:

> "We ourselves, who are Jews by birth and not Gentile sinners, yet who know that a man is not justified by works of the law but through faith in Jesus Christ, even we have believed in Christ Jesus, in order to be justified by faith in Christ, and not by works of the law, because by works of the law shall no one be justified." (Gal. 2:15–16)

As Udo Schaefer, the author of *The Light Shineth in Darkness*, notes in his discussion of Paul's polemic against law, it was from Paul's theology, not from Christ's, that much of future Christianity would derive its system of beliefs (95–97). And because Paul's interpretation largely determined the future course of Christian thought, much of contemporary Christianity accepts the doctrine that Christ and God are the same entity and that Christ's martyrdom was sufficient payment for the salvation of man. One tract states the belief succinctly as follows:

> You can do nothing to earn eternal life. It is not our work that saves us, but Faith in the Lord Jesus Christ. You do not receive Eternal life by working for it or by trying to make yourself behave. Accept the payment He has made for your sins and you can rest and be assured you have eternal life.*

---

*This is a portion of a tract left on my windshield some years ago. I have since lost the tract but had written down the text because it seemed to me such a forthright statement of this doctrine.

Less adamant but essentially the same is the response of respected contemporary fundamentalist Dr. Billy Graham to the question of salvation through grace. He affirms that we cannot earn salvation or even appreciably alter our spiritual condition through deeds, but he does acknowledge that the state of salvation will inevitably be reflected in our daily actions. In responding to the question why a Christian should "bother to be good if our goodness doesn't get us into heaven," Dr. Graham states:

> God loves you so much that his Son was willing to die for you, so you could be saved. If you really understand something of how deep God's love is for you, you cannot be indifferent to him. You will want to love him in return. And how do you show your love for him? By seeking to live the way he wants you to live. ("My Answer")

For the Bahá'í, recognizing the Manifestations and appreciating the absolutely essential nature of their sacrifices for the sake of our salvation and enlightenment is likewise essential, but it is not sufficient. Hand in hand with recognizing the Prophets and acknowledging their exalted station and exemplary life must go exacting obedience to the laws and ordinances that they reveal for our guidance. Our physical lives, therefore, are not simply reflections of belief or embellishments of faith. They are in this life the primary ingredients of and requisites for faith. Bahá'u'lláh puts it succinctly in the Kitáb-i-Aqdas when He states: "These twin duties are inseparable. Neither is acceptable without the other" (Synopsis 11).

The Bahá'í writings do not disagree with Boethius' overall observation that universal justice is being wrought over a period of time. Neither does the Bahá'í point of view disagree with the idea that as individuals we may have to await the next life before we see justice done in our lives. But the Bahá'í perspective about the just purposes of and proper attitude toward physical reality differs radically from the views of the Christian stoics who found in Boethius' work support for their rejection of the vita activa.

A Bahá'í Response to Milton

Milton's examination of justice in the physical world is in many ways much more complete and complex than Boethius' work, and the Bahá'í writings confirm many of Milton's basic conclusions.

As we have already observed, Milton's work upholds the doctrine of free will, whether it leads to successes or failures. In this sense Milton's theology does not seem obsessed with the doctrine of man's fall from grace. Instead, Milton portrays Edenic bliss as inferior to the possibilities of freely chosen ascent after the Fall. He does not mean that disobedience is good in and of itself, but he does imply that struggling for spiritual perfection produces a state of development that is superior to childlike innocence. 'Abdu'l-Bahá describes clearly the importance of free will in spiritual development when He makes a similar distinction between two types of spiritual perfection:

> The hearts of all children are of the utmost purity. They are mirrors upon which no dust has fallen. But this purity is on account of weakness and innocence, not on account of any strength and testing, for as this is the early period of their childhood, their hearts and minds are unsullied by the world. They cannot display any great intelligence. They have neither hypocrisy nor deceit. This is on account of the child's weakness, whereas the man becomes pure through his strength. Through the power of intelligence he becomes simple; through the great power of reason and understanding and not through the power of weakness he becomes sincere. (*Promulgation* 53)

Bahá'u'lláh likewise asserts this principle when He states: "All that which ye potentially possess can, however, be manifested only as a result of your own volition. Your own acts testify to this truth" (*Gleanings* 149).

A second important similarity between Milton's conclusions and the teachings of the Bahá'í Faith regards the concept of sin. As a Puritan, Milton might be expected to espouse a belief in primal sin—a belief that man inherits his sinfulness because of the fall from grace—especially since his topic is the Adamic myth. The thrust of Puritan theology as devised by Calvin derives largely from

Pauline Christianity, and Paul observes that sin entered the world because of Adam and that man is saved by accepting Christ's sacrifice (Rom. 5:12–19). Milton, however, consistently portrays sin as a process that occurs when there is a witting rebellion against just law or authority, a failure to abide by "right reason" (12.84). In the same way Bahá'u'lláh states that "every good thing is of God, and every evil thing is from yourselves" (*Gleanings* 149); 'Abdu'l-Bahá likewise states that "in the choice of good and bad actions he is free, and he commits them according to his will" (*Some Answered Questions* 248).

Milton thus portrays Satan as tempter, as a miserable spirit who wishes to make others as miserable as he; but Satan is not in any significant way the source of sin. He tempts Adam and Eve with choices, but the choices were already there, and the flaws in the characters of Adam and Eve were ready to be exploited. Eve wants to become godlike. Adam is too concerned with pleasing His wife. Satan is so full of pride that he cannot abide submitting to any authority, even a just one, even though he knows he would be happier were he to comply. These weaknesses are not equivalent to sin itself; everyone has weakness. Sin occurs when one yields to unhealthy desires instead of following the dictates of reason.

A third important similarity between Milton's theodicy and the Bahá'í perspective is in the doctrine of grace or forgiveness. Milton implies that the only way God's creatures can become bereft of redemption is through a willful rejection of grace. Alone and aware of what he has lost, Milton's Satan asks himself, "Is there no place / Left for repentance, none for pardon left?" Satan answers his own query when he observes, "None left but by submission. . . . " (4.79–81). Since he refuses to submit, forgiveness is unavailable to him. Stated another way, he refuses to avail himself of grace, and God will not impose grace on him.

The Bahá'í writings also assert that we are never beyond redemption unless we persist in rejecting it:

> The portals of grace are wide open before the face of all men. . . . No man that seeketh Us will We ever disappoint, neither shall he that hath set his face towards Us be denied access unto Our court. . . . " (Bahá'u'lláh, *Gleanings* 271–72)

A fourth Miltonic doctrine that parallels a significant Bahá'í belief is the concept that heaven and hell are internal spiritual conditions. The angel Michael explains to Adam and Eve that if they follow his advice by adding deeds to their knowledge, they will "possess/A paradise within" (12.586–87) superior to the Edenic bliss they must abandon. Paradise is portrayed as an internal condition of enlightenment, a proximity to God, a compliance with His ordinances.

Milton's hell is also a metaphysical condition. Although hell in this fictional work is described as a physical abode, the important suffering for Satan results not from the torments of a dreadful place but from his internal anguish at having been deprived of heaven and of his lofty position as archangel.

The Bahá'í writings express in a number of places the same notion of heaven and hell as internal states of being. In the Tablet of Ishráqát we find the following: "They say: 'Where is Paradise, and where is Hell?' Say: 'The one is reunion with Me; the other thine own self, O thou who dost associate a partner with God and doubtest'" (Bahá'u'lláh, *Tablets of Bahá'u'lláh* 118). 'Abdu'l-Bahá states that the "paradise and hell of existence are found in all the worlds of God, whether in this world or in the spiritual heavenly worlds" (*Some Answered Questions* 223). Our experience in the afterlife may be substantially different from what we experience in the physical world, but 'Abdu'l-Bahá does imply that, since the important criteria for assessing our felicity are internal and spiritual, the just rewards of spiritual development can be experienced in earthly life as well as in the afterlife, as can the punishment for our failure to live according to God's will.

Finally, besides Milton's justification of God's actions through his delineation of man's free will as the agent for his downfall is Milton's portrayal of history as a process by which mankind will be redeemed and educated. This long-range view of history as a divine process is at the heart of Milton's theology, just as the Bahá'í belief in progressive revelation is the cornerstone of Bahá'í theology.

As we have noted, Boethius affirms that history is being subtly influenced by divine providence, but he implies, as Alexander Pope does some fourteen hundred years later, that the eternal process of history is veiled from man and is, therefore, not properly a human concern: "Know then thyself, presume not God to scan;/The proper study of mankind is Man" (*An Essay on Man*, in *Norton Anthology* 1:2250). But in Milton's theology God is not only personally aware of and concerned with the just operation of His creation; He reveals to Adam and Eve through Michael the plan by which justice will be wrought in history. In effect, God intervenes in the present and explains how He intends to intervene in the future to bring about beneficial results from these historical events. Furthermore, we infer from Michael's instruction that it is important for every human being to be aware of the mechanics of God's plan for redeeming mankind so that everyone can participate in facilitating the result.

These, then, are some of the ways that Milton's theodicy seems generally in compliance with the Bahá'í writings. It is even accurate to say that Milton takes traditional Christian theology about as far as it can go by way of justifying God's placement of His creation in a physical world. Physical reality is depicted as a place of learning, an environment in which humanity will in time achieve understanding of God's justice and mercy.

The major difference between Milton's explanation of physical reality as an expression of divine justice and the Bahá'í perspective of physical reality results primarily from the traditional Christian perception of Christ's revelation as a unique intervention in history. Indeed, the Bahá'í principle of progressive revelation (the equality and succession of the Prophets) is at the heart of all Bahá'í theology and is the sine qua non in any successful attempt at theodicy.

Milton avoids the usual Christian basis for a belief in the uniqueness of Christ—he portrays the Son as essentially distinct from God and not part of a Trinity (not of the same essence). But he does not avoid the myriad logical problems that result from perceiving the advent of Christ as the sole occasion in human history for the revelation of God's perfection. Milton does not explain, therefore, why a God Who is like a loving parent would give His children only one opportunity to be redeemed. Christ Himself never stated that His advent was the unique revelation from God nor that He was the last appearance of such a spiritualizing force. Indeed, He frequently chided the Jews for having perpetrated in the past what they were about to recommit by persecuting Him:

"Therefore I send you prophets and wise men and scribes, some of whom you will kill and crucify, and some you will scourge in your synagogues and persecute from town to town. . . . " (Matt. 23:34)

In fact, Christ clearly proclaims His mission as fulfilling the revelations of the past and as setting the stage for the appearance of future Manifestations. Regarding the past Prophets He states, "Think not that I have come to abolish the law and the prophets; I have come not to abolish them but to fulfil them" (Matt. 5:17). Regarding the awareness of the past Prophets of His own coming to fulfill their work, Christ says, "Your father Abraham rejoiced that he was to see my day; he saw it and was glad" (John 8:56).

These and similar statements by Christ call to mind a number of important Bahá'í beliefs about the relationship among the Manifestations. First, the Manifestations are fully aware of each other and build upon each other's efforts, each being cognizant of how His particular ministry takes up where the previous revelation left off. Each likewise is aware that the scope of His own revelation is limited to what the people are able to understand for a particular duration of time. Thus Christ clearly indicates that another Manifestation will build upon the foundation He has laid:

"I have yet many things to say to you, but you cannot bear them now. When the Spirit of truth comes, he will guide you into all the truth; for he will not speak on his own authority, but whatever he hears he will speak, and he will declare to you the things that are to come." (John 16:12–13)

Second, the Prophets or Manifestations are immaculate in their lives and come with power and authority which results from the fact that, as Christ notes in the previous passage, each speaks "whatever he hears." As Christ often explained, He acted not on His own authority but relinquished His own will to do the bidding of God:

"The words that I say to you I do not speak on my own authority; but the Father who dwells in me does his works." (John 14:10)

"He who believes in me, believes not in me but in him who sent me."
(John 12:44)

"For I have not spoken on my own authority; the Father who sent me
has himself given me commandment what to say and what to speak.
And I know that his commandment is eternal life. What I say,
therefore, I say as the Father has bidden me." (John 12:49–50)

Third, when Christ states that He existed before Abraham's
appearance, He is alluding to one aspect of the special nature of
these Prophets: They are not spiritualized human beings. Their
spiritual nature is superior to that of the human soul, and in fact,
unlike human beings they are preexistent. Shoghi Effendi explains:
"The Prophets, unlike us, are pre-existent. The soul of Christ
existed in the spiritual world before His birth in this world" (*High
Endeavours* 71).

The Bahá'í concept of the unity and continuity of prophecy
deriving from the successive appearances of immaculate and
divinely empowered souls is the most vital and fundamental
ingredient in any attempt to justify God's ways to humanity and to
explain why a loving God would place His creation in a physical
world. Without such a concept no explanation of physical reality or
God's justice can make complete or final sense. For if we accept the
notion that God has devised physical reality as a place of learning
and has further established that man cannot succeed without
assistance, it would make little sense for God to deprive mankind of
sufficient guidance to accomplish the task of human transformation
or to await some particular moment in history to begin the process
of salvation. Rather, it is logical that a just and loving God, like a
loving parent, would bestow that guidance from the beginning and
would never withhold it.

Of course, we cannot much blame Milton for believing that
Christ was God's sole revelator—he inherited this misinterpretation
of religious history from over a thousand years of imbedded dogma.
Most important, he, like most of Western Christendom, was
deprived of the illumination which Muḥammad's revelation shed
on this subject. One of the dominant themes of the Qur'án is the

enunciation of divine assistance which God has given to man through the succession of Manifestations. Muḥammad frequently alludes to the lives of the Prophets and the pitiful irony of their rejection by mankind:

> Moreover, to Moses gave we "the Book," and we raised up apostles after him; and to Jesus, son of Mary, gave we clear proofs of *his mission*, and strengthened him by the Holy Spirit. So oft then as an apostle cometh to you with that which your souls desire not, swell ye with pride, and treat some as impostors, and slay others? (Qur'án 2:81)

Muḥammad spoke directly to the Christian misinterpretations of Christ's station and ministry when He rebuked those who had come to believe that Christ was God or that Christ was the Son in the flesh of God (that He was the same essence):

> Believe therefore in God and his apostles, and say not, "Three:" (there is a Trinity)—Forbear—it will be better for you. God is only one God! Far be it from His glory that He should have a son. . . .
> The Messiah disdaineth not to be a servant of God, nor do the angels who are nigh unto Him. (Qur'án 4.169–70)

The importance of the concept of progressive revelation to the Bahá'í beliefs is partially demonstrated by the fact that, next to the Kitáb-i-Aqdas, the most important single work revealed by Bahá'-u'lláh is the Kitáb-i-Íqán, an exquisitely organized and lucid exposition on this subject.* In the Kitáb-i-Íqán Bahá'u'lláh explains how all of the Manifestations are "sent down from the heaven of the

---

*Shoghi Effendi states, "A model of Persian prose, of a style at once original, chaste and vigorous, and remarkably lucid, both cogent in argument and matchless in its irresistible eloquence, this Book, setting forth in outline the Grand Redemptive Scheme of God, occupies a position unequalled by any work in the entire range of Bahá'í literature, except the Kitáb-i-Aqdas, Bahá'u'lláh's Most Holy Book" (*God Passes By* 138–39).

Will of God, and as they all arise to proclaim His irresistible Faith, they therefore are regarded as one soul and the same person" (*Kitáb-i-Íqán* 152).

Still another noteworthy distinction between the implications of Milton's theology and Bahá'í beliefs has to do with the interpretation of the Adamic myth. As 'Abdu'l-Bahá notes in *Some Answered Questions* (122–26), many interpretations of the Edenic story are possible, but what is indisputable from a Bahá'í point of view is the belief that Adam was in reality a Prophet of God, a Manifestation. In the Qur'án, for example, Muḥammad describes Adam as revealing the essentially spiritual nature of the physical world. Although the Book of Genesis seems to portray a literal man giving names to birds and beasts and "every living creature" (2:19), possibly a myth alluding to the beginning of language, the Qur'án portrays Adam as a Prophet whose task it is to reveal to the phenomenal world its spiritual attributes:

> They said, "Praise be to Thee! We have no knowledge but what Thou hast given us to know. Thou! Thou art the Knowing, the Wise." He said, "O Adam, inform them of their names." And when he had informed them of their names, He said, "Did I not say to you that I know the hidden things of the Heavens and of the Earth, and that I know what ye bring to light, and what ye hide?" (2:30–31)

Here Adam does not name things in creation; He "informs them" of names they already possess. In so doing, He implies that the name is not so much a literal appellation as it is a spiritual quality, recalling for us our earlier examination of the doctrine espoused by Plato. The Qur'anic explanation is further suggested in the Bahá'í writings, where the use of the term *name* denotes spiritual attributes (Bahá'u'lláh, *Gleanings* 22, 48, 65, 165) and the term *Kingdom of Names* refers to the physical world (*Gleanings* 184, 195), a place where spiritual reality is invested with physical form:

> Inasmuch as He, the sovereign Lord of all, hath willed to reveal His sovereignty in the kingdom of names and attributes, each and every created thing hath, through the act of the Divine Will, been made a sign of His glory. So pervasive and general is this revelation that

nothing whatsoever in the whole universe can be discovered that doth not reflect His splendor. (Bahá'u'lláh, *Gleanings* 184).

In the Bahá'í writings the spiritual world is sometimes referred to as the "world of vision," as a reality in which the attributes are no longer concealed in physical forms: "The Kingdom is the world of vision . . . , where all the concealed realities will become disclosed" ('Abdu'l-Bahá, *Tablets of Abdul-Baha Abbas* 1:205).

The Bahá'í interpretation of the Adamic myth does not directly contravene anything Milton is attempting to say, but it does give a more ample explanation about why humankind is ordained to begin life in a physical environment. In Milton's interpretation the earthly home is partly punishment for Adam's transgression, but mostly, we come to understand, a means by which humankind will come to appreciate God's mercy and grandeur.

As we will see in our more ample examination of the Bahá'í paradigm of physical reality, the Bahá'í writings portray the physical world and our experience in this subtle environment as valuable in and of itself; it is not merely a matter of making the best of a bad situation. For while we now have an idea of the basic problems in discerning justice in physical reality, as well as the Bahá'í response to some of the major questions raised by previous attempts to search for justice in the physical world, we are now ready to assemble a model, or paradigm, of physical creation as we are able to infer it from the Bahá'í scriptures.

The Bahá'í Paradigm of Physical Reality   2

The world, indeed each existing being, proclaims to us one of the names of God, but the reality of man is the collective reality, the general reality, and is the center where the glory of all the perfections of God shine forth—that is to say, for each name, each attribute, each perfection which we affirm of God there exists a sign in man.

—'Abdu'l-Bahá

Having examined the Bahá'í response to some of the major questions that arise out of the traditional attempts to discover the workings of physical reality, we may now have some sense of how the Bahá'í writings explain and justify the spiritual purposes of the physical world. But before we can go beyond these beliefs to determine what practical effect they have on our daily lives, we need to approach the Bahá'í theory of physical creation in a more complete and orderly fashion. By assembling in a logical order the essential ingredients of the Bahá'í theoretical paradigm of physical reality, we can better appreciate why a physical existence has been devised by the Creator as the initial stage of development for essentially spiritual beings.

The Creator

The Bahá'í paradigm of physical reality logically begins with the concept of God as Creator. Because God is "immensely exalted beyond every human attribute" and "will remain in His Reality everlastingly hidden from the sight of men" (Bahá'u'lláh, *Kitáb-i-*

Íqán 98), we are, especially in physical life, limited in what we can understand about the Creator. We know God through the Manifestations and through physical reality itself. As perfect reflections of the qualities of the Creator, the Manifestations dramatize God's spiritual image to us in their actions and reveal His guidance through words and laws. Physical reality likewise displays for us indirectly through analogues and symbols the qualities of the Creator.

In spite of our limited understanding of God, there are other noteworthy inferences we can draw from the Bahá'í writings about God. For example, it is clear that *God* is not simply a term designating the sum total of universal forces and attributes. The Bahá'í concept of the Deity envisions a Being Who is independent of His creation but is cognitive, caring, and concerned for His creation and its progress. For this reason He guides creation toward fulfillment. It is also clear that God wishes to express His love by creating beings capable of understanding His attributes and manifesting that understanding in action:

> Veiled in My immemorial being and in the ancient eternity of My essence, I knew My love for thee; therefore I created thee, have engraved on thee Mine image and revealed to thee My beauty. (Bahá'u'lláh, *Hidden Words* 4)

Hence Bahá'u'lláh states that, although people differ in capacity, God "hath endowed every soul with the capacity to recognize the signs of God" (*Gleanings* 105–06).

Here, then, is the essence of our relationship to the Creator: that in physical life we come to know Him indirectly through our knowledge of the Manifestations and their teachings and through the "signs" or attributes of God as they are manifested in the Kingdom of Names (in physical reality). We then attempt to acquire those attributes by giving them dramatic expression in our daily lives.

The relationship and arrangement between God and humanity does not imply that we are remote or removed from God. The more we study and emulate the qualities of the Creator, the more we understand Him. Furthermore, the Manifestations as reflections of that divine reality so perfectly manifest the characteristics of God immanent in them that to study and understand them and their teachings is tantamount, in earthly life, to proximity to God:

> Were any of the all-embracing Manifestations of God to declare: "I am God!" He verily speaketh the truth, and no doubt attacheth thereto. For it hath been repeatedly demonstrated that through their Revelation, their attributes and names, the Revelation of God, His name and His attributes, are made manifest in the world. (Bahá'u'-lláh, *Kitáb-i-Íqán* 178)

Physical Creation as Divine Emanation

The next ingredient in constructing the Bahá'í paradigm is creation itself. Here we need to establish three major points: Physical creation has always existed; physical creation is in a continual state of flux; and physical creation serves to reflect the qualities of the Creator.

The first point—that physical creation has no beginning—is the most controversial in light of the ongoing debate between the evolutionists and the "creationists." And yet the Bahá'í point of view regarding the eternality of physical existence is as simple as it is logical. Stated plainly, the Bahá'í teachings reject the views of both the creationists and the evolutionists as their theories are commonly presented. Instead, the Bahá'í writings affirm that since God has no beginning, and since one of His appellations is "the Creator," there has never been a time when creation did not exist. In other words, we cannot conceive of a Creator without a creation:

> The Creator always had a creation; the rays have always shone and gleamed from the reality of the sun, for without the rays the sun would be opaque darkness. The names and attributes of God require the existence of beings, and the Eternal Bounty does not cease. If it were to, it would be contrary to the perfections of God. (*Some Answered Questions* 281)

As another proof of the eternality of creation 'Abdu'l-Bahá notes that absolute existence cannot come from absolute nonexistence. And since something cannot come from nothing, creation has always existed (281).

Of course, we know from scientific evidence, as well as what we can glean from religious myths such as the story of creation recounted in Genesis, that particular worlds or planets do have a beginning and do pass through myriad stages of evolutionary growth and development. In this sense there is, from our perspective on this planet, a beginning, a creation. In reality, however, we are observing in such a process a second Bahá'í principle about physical creation—it is in a continual stage of dynamic change. All physical compositions are always coming into being or going out of being in a structural sense; they are impermanent arrangements. Therefore, when we talk of creation on earth, we are talking about the way in which matter combined over time to assume certain properties.

But 'Abdu'l-Bahá explains that material creation itself is a single substance, and that substance has no beginning and no end: "Then it is evident that in the beginning matter was one, and that one matter appeared in different aspects in each element" (*Some Answered Questions* 181). Worlds may come into being and go out of being, but physical reality is a perpetual and eternal organism that does not diminish:

> Therefore, as the Essence of Unity (that is, the existence of God) is everlasting and eternal—that is to say, it has neither beginning nor end—it is certain that this world of existence, this endless universe, has neither beginning nor end. Yes, it may be that one of the parts of the universe, one of the globes, for example, may come into existence, or may be disintegrated, but the other globes are still existing; the universe would not be disordered nor destroyed. (*Some Answered Questions* 180)

The planet earth, like every other physical composition, "must of necessity be decomposed" (*Some Answered Questions* 181) after it has achieved its fruition and fulfilled its purpose. That purpose may be likened to the purpose of all other organic entities in the physical world—gradually to reflect in greater degrees the qualities of the Creator.

In fact, in a significant explanation of universal structure 'Abdu'l-Bahá explains that larger universal entities resemble in structure and evolution the minuscule particles of creation, "for both are subjected to one natural system, one universal law and divine organization":

> So you will find the smallest atoms in the universal system are similar to the greatest beings of the universe. It is clear that they come into existence from one laboratory of might under one natural system and one universal law; therefore, they may be compared to one another. (*Some Answered Questions* 182)

We can observe, therefore, a similarity between the evolutionary growth of a seed into a flourishing plant and the development of a man from conception to maturity, or between the evolving physical aspect of man on the planet and the spiritual development of human society. The parallels are endless, but one of the most illuminating is 'Abdu'l-Bahá's comparison of the evolution of our planet to a seed growing in the matrix of the universe:

> In the same manner, it is evident that this terrestrial globe, having once found existence, grew and developed in the matrix of the universe, and came forth in different forms and conditions, until gradually it attained this present perfection, and became adorned with innumerable beings, and appeared as a finished organization. (*Some Answered Questions* 182–83)

There are, of course, milestones in the process of evolution, whether we are examining the geological changes of the earth, the religious history of mankind, or our own individual progress, and we need to be able to describe these stages of growth. We speak of times of beginning and ending not as absolutes but as points of crucial change in relation to other events. So it was that the ancient peoples used the Adamic myth as a symbol of some milestone in the evolving of human awareness about concepts of morality. But when religions interpret biblical passages about creation as literal beginnings of the physical world, they fail to appreciate what these myths are depicting. The same holds true for biblical and Qur'anic prophecies about the "time of the end" and the "Last Judgment." Instead of alluding to a destruction of physical reality, these phrases are referring to major points of transition in the spiritual evolving of one planet—the end of one phase of growth and the beginning of another, just as adolescence might be considered a traumatic termination of childhood, or as the birth of a child might be viewed as the end of life in the womb.

The Bahá'í writings, therefore, offer the evolutionists and creationists a new definition of "creation," either as it regards the origins of life on this planet or as it pertains to the continuity of the universe as a whole. Things have a beginning: matter assumes a certain arrangement or combination to form the human organism, or to fashion geological structures, or even to form our planet or whole planetary systems. But creation as a whole is eternal.

A third major principle of physical creation is that it is an emanation of the Creator in the same way that rays of light emanate from the sun. From a Bahá'í point of view God is not dependent on physical creation. He does not need or require its success for His own well-being; rather, the reverse is true:

> The sun in its own essence is independent of the bodies which it lights, for its light is in itself and is free and independent of the terrestrial globe; so the earth is under the influence of the sun and receives its light, whereas the sun and its rays are entirely independent of the earth. But if there were no sun, the earth and all earthly beings could not exist. ('Abdu'l-Bahá, *Some Answered Questions* 202)

The relationship of the physical world to the spiritual world is summarized succinctly in the Hidden Word which states: "Out of the wastes of nothingness, with the clay of My command I made thee to appear, and have ordained for thy training every atom in existence and the essence of all created things" (Bahá'u'lláh, *Hidden Words* 32).

Because the physical world is a reflection of the unseen spiritual realm, it has as its animating and essential nature the capacity to reflect the attributes of that realm. The primacy of the spiritual world in this relationship is stated powerfully by 'Abdu'l-Bahá when He observes that the spiritual realm "is the real world, and this nether place is only its shadow stretching out. A shadow hath no life of its own; its existence is only a fantasy, and nothing more; it is but images reflected in water, and seeming as pictures to the eye" (*Selections* 178).

The Fruit of Creation

Considering the organic nature of the created universe as an expression of the spiritual world, we might think it erroneous to distinguish one part of the physical world as having primary importance since the whole system is organized by and unified around the same purpose—the reflection of spiritual principles. But the next ingredient in the paradigm of physical creation is the Bahá'í belief that the spiritual education of humankind is the end product of this divinely empowered mechanism.

'Abdu'l-Bahá explains the station of humanity by comparing physical reality to a fruit tree and mankind to the fruit itself:

> If there were no man, the perfections of the spirit would not appear, and the light of the mind would not be resplendent in this world. This world would be like a body without a soul.
>
>   This world is also in the condition of a fruit tree, and man is like the fruit; without fruit the tree would be useless. (*Some Answered Questions* 201)

There are at least two reasons why humankind has such an exalted place in the physical world. First, while all creation reflects the attributes of the Creator, only we are capable of reflecting each of these attributes. Second, only we are endowed with the capacity to comprehend our relationship with God, to appreciate its significance, and to decide whether we will fulfill our potential by incorporating God's attributes into our actions.

But what gives us the capacity to reflect those attributes? What enables us to do what animals and the rest of physical creation cannot? We could cite the capacity we have to think abstractly together with whatever distinctions we can observe empirically, but all of these distinctions result from the soul, an entity which humankind possesses uniquely among the rest of physical creation:

> Know, verily, that the soul is a sign of God, a heavenly gem whose reality the most learned of men hath failed to grasp, and whose mystery no mind, however acute, can ever hope to unravel. It is the first among all created things to declare the excellence of its Creator, the first to recognize His glory, to cleave to His truth, and to bow down in adoration before Him. (Bahá'u'lláh, *Gleanings* 158–59)

What we can know about the soul is limited, but we do know that this animating force is responsible for our other special human faculties, such as thought and will. We further know that alone among creation the human soul has a beginning but no end. It takes its beginning when it associates with the body at conception, and it endures eternally beyond this association.

Another fundamental verity about humankind as the fruit of physical creation is the Bahá'í concept of evolution. According to the Bahá'í writings the human being has not evolved from other, lower forms of life. The human physical form has evolved, just as an embryo may at first appear to be a tadpole or may later assume various other forms of life. But only the human embryo will, upon reaching fruition, become a human being. In the same way, the human species may at one time in its evolution have appeared to be similar in form to other species, but the human species has always been a distinct creation:

> The beginning of the existence of man on the terrestrial globe resembles his formation in the womb of the mother. The embryo in the womb of the mother gradually grows and develops until birth, after which it continues to grow and develop until it reaches the age of discretion and maturity. Though in infancy the signs of the mind and spirit appear in man, they do not reach the degree of perfection; they are imperfect. Only when man attains maturity do the mind and the spirit appear and become evident in utmost perfection. ('Abdu'l-Bahá, *Some Answered Questions* 198)

Not only has the human species always been unique on this

planet; the Bahá'í writings also indicate that, since humankind is the essential product and raison d'être of creation, humankind has always existed. Put another way, since physical creation is a perfect creation and since humankind is the perfection or fruit of that creation, humanity has always existed somewhere in the physical universe; otherwise, the creation would be imperfect. 'Abdu'l-Bahá explains that inasmuch as "the universe has no imperfection" (*Some Answered Questions* 177), and since man is the "chief member" of the body of the universe (*Some Answered Questions* 178), there has never been a time when man did not exist:

> We consider man . . . the sum of all existing perfections. When we speak of man, we mean the perfect one, the foremost individual in the world, who is the sum of spiritual and apparent perfections, and who is like the sun among the beings. Then imagine that at one time the sun did not exist, but that it was a planet; surely at such a time the relations of existence would be disordered. How can such a thing be imagined? (*Some Answered Questions* 178).

Finally, as we will discuss later in more detail, we observe in the Bahá'í writings that each individual has an essential part to play in the process of fulfilling human potential. Bahá'u'lláh states that the "perfection" which enables us to reflect all the attributes of God is only a perfection of capacity until we freely choose to make that potentiality a reality (*Gleanings* 149). In man "are potentially revealed all the attributes and names of God to a degree that no other created being hath excelled or surpassed" (*Gleanings* 177). For that potentiality to become a reality, other ingredients of our system, both internal and external to man, must be added.

Salvation as Motion

If mankind is the fruit of physical creation, the next component of our model of physical reality would logically be whatever constitutes human fulfillment. According to most religions the appropriate goal of human endeavors in physical life is the attainment of salvation. What constitutes salvation varies from religion to religion, but the most commonly held belief is the concept of a precise division between those who achieve fulfillment and those who do not. The "saved" go to heaven; the "unsaved" go to hell. The Bahá'í concept of human justice in this larger sense of human fulfillment or fruition is substantially different from the views of Jews, Christians, and Muslims, or at least from how these views are most often professed.

For one thing, the Bahá'í writings affirm that human spiritual progress is not confined to the physical world. Progress in the Kingdom of Names is distinct in several ways from progress in the spiritual realm, but in either world there is no single point of salvation. All progress is relative; all spiritual attainment is relative. What might be exalted spiritual advancement for one soul might be regressive for another. Since each of us advances in relation to a myriad influences, opportunities, and obstacles, a true assessment of spiritual achievement must perforce be veiled to all except an infinitely knowledgeable being.

If our awareness, our individuality, and our development continue in the spiritual realm from where we leave off in the physical world, there is no point at which the spiritual evolution of the human soul is completed. There may be stages of attainment —the gaining of certitude, for example. But the human soul is capable both in this life and in the next of infinite progress, even though there is never change in our essential nature—the human soul will always remain a human soul:

> Both before and after putting off this material form, there is progress in perfection but not in state. So beings are consummated in perfect man. There is no other being higher than a perfect man. But man when he has reached this state can still make progress in perfections but not in state because there is no state higher than that of a perfect man to which he can transfer himself. He only progresses in the state of humanity, for the human perfections are infinite. ('Abdu'l-Bahá, *Some Answered Questions* 237)

The importance of the belief in salvation as motion cannot be exaggerated. It implies, for one thing, that our physical experience is but the beginning of an endless educational process. Doubtless the process changes as we change, just as the methods of learning for an elementary-school child might differ radically from those of a postdoctoral student.

To some the Bahá'í concept of human fruition might seem logical and refreshing, offering as it does an eternity of challenge and growth rather than a single leap of faith followed by the prospect of dwelling endlessly in celestial stasis. To others the Bahá'í concept might seem to imply being doomed to the eternal frustration of pursuing an unattainable goal. But the latter inference is based on the traditional concept of salvation as a finished or completed state, whereas the Bahá'í concept envisions salvation as motion itself, the profound joy of being in motion toward godliness. Human satisfaction or fulfillment does not, therefore, await some future point of achievement, any more than gaining knowledge awaits a finished point of understanding before learning brings rewards. The process of learning is itself enjoyable and always relative.

The initial stages of learning (or "the learning curve," as it is sometimes called) may be steep and difficult, but once motion is attained, the rewards are infinite. In short, the human soul in motion has achieved its fundamental objective. Its long-term goal is to sustain that progress. This is the Bahá'í concept of the just purpose and just condition of the individual, and of society as a whole.

From such a perspective, life in heaven as it is often portrayed by the teachings of other religions—a physical place of comfort and ease—would seem to be an experience quickly doomed to utter boredom. A truly heavenly condition would more likely involve an endless progression of fulfillment and enlightenment.

The implications of the Bahá'í concept of justice as motion are extremely important to all other parts of the paradigm. Education in such a system cannot be based solely on creating a fixed pattern of behavior in an individual or in conveying a body of facts. Educational systems must be capable of flexibility and growth in order to minister to the requirements of constantly changing individuals. What was just, appropriate, and fulfilling for someone yesterday may be unjust for that same individual today. The same principle applies equally well to those institutions which minister to the needs of society as a whole, since human society is evolutionary in nature: Bahá'u'lláh states that "all men have been created to carry forward an ever-advancing civilization" (*Gleanings* 215). Therefore, institutions whose function it is to foster this progress must themselves be capable of growth. For example, 'Abdu'l-Bahá notes that religion itself must respond to the changing exigencies of the human condition:

> Religion is the outer expression of the divine reality. Therefore, it must be living, vitalized, moving and progressive. If it be without motion and nonprogressive, it is without the divine life; it is dead. The divine institutes are continuously active and evolutionary; therefore, the revelation of them must be progressive and continuous. (*Promulgation* 140)

The Prerequisite of Autonomy

Since motion toward perfection is the Bahá'í definition of salvation and fulfillment, in both the physical and the spiritual worlds, we need to consider how that motion is achieved and sustained from without and from within. But first we need to acknowledge an essential attribute of that motion and a major ingredient in the Bahá'í paradigm of physical reality—the autonomy of human advancement.

On the simplest level we can understand autonomy by again using the example of the training of a child. A youth may be trained to behave well, to exhibit manners, kindness, morality. Certainly these attributes are desirable. But the important progress of the young soul is taking place when that motion toward human perfection becomes freely chosen, self-sustained, autonomous. This requisite does not mean that teaching a child to mimic proper behavior is in any way wrong—one of the surest ways for us to become noble is to pretend we are and act accordingly. But it does imply that human justice or salvation must ultimately derive from each individual's conscious striving. The quality of human ascent, the just or proper condition of the human being, is what Bahá'u'lláh alludes to when He states that by the aid of justice "thou shalt see with thine own eyes and not through the eyes of others, and shalt know of thine own knowledge and not through the knowledge of thy neighbor" (*Hidden Words* 4).

Without autonomy of motion, we may confuse brainwashing with conviction, blind imitation with faith and belief. To protect humanity from these mistaken attitudes, Bahá'u'lláh ensured that each person who becomes a Bahá'í must do so by his or her own choice—one cannot inherit the Bahá'í Faith. Likewise, in teaching the Bahá'í Faith, Bahá'ís are admonished not to "contend with any one" so that if someone responds to the teachings, "he will have responded to his own behoof. . . . " (*Gleanings* 279). 'Abdu'l-Bahá reiterates this same principle: "Do not argue with anyone, and be wary of disputation. Speak out the truth. If your hearer accepteth, the aim is achieved" (qtd. in Bahá'u'lláh et al., *Individual and Teaching* 13).

But deterrents to autonomy of motion are not always externally caused, not always involuntary. Equally detrimental to independence of thought is imitation, the relegating of our own free choices to the opinions or decisions of others. Not only does such abandonment of human responsibility allow the iniquitous to mislead mankind; on a personal level imitation is the source of all prejudice.

In the Bahá'í writings imitation is denounced as the antithesis of justice and the source of human degradation. In the Kitáb-i-Íqán Bahá'u'lláh describes imitation as one of the most persistent evils afflicting religion: "Consider how men for generations have been blindly imitating their fathers, and have been trained according to such ways and manners as have been laid down by the dictates of their Faith" (*Kitáb-i-Íqán* 74). 'Abdu'l-Bahá goes so far as to cite imitation as one cause of the decline of religion itself:

> Imitation destroys the foundation of religion, extinguishes the spirituality of the human world, transforms heavenly illumination into darkness and deprives man of the knowledge of God. It is the cause of the victory of materialism and infidelity over religion; it is the denial of Divinity and the law of revelation; it refuses Prophethood and rejects the Kingdom of God. (*Promulgation* 161)

Bahá'u'lláh forcefully summarizes the fundamental nature of

autonomy when He states with unmistakable clarity that since each individual has the capacity to recognize divine attributes, everyone is ultimately responsible for his own spiritual condition:

> every man hath been, and will continue to be, able of himself to appreciate the Beauty of God, the Glorified. Had he not been endowed with such a capacity, how could he be called to account for his failure? . . . For the faith of no man can be conditioned by any one except himself. (*Gleanings* 143)

External Assistance

As we noted in our comparison of the Bahá'í view of physical creation with that presented in *Paradise Lost,* the most essential and distinguishing characteristic of the Bahá'í concept of a justly functioning creation is the progressive and unremitting assistance provided for human advancement. Because the ceaseless motion toward perfection must be autonomous, it might seem that external assistance would prohibit independence. But while the final responsibility for spiritual growth devolves upon the individual, human progress, whether individual or collective, is impossible without some sort of external guidance. 'Abdu'l-Bahá states, "A man who has not had a spiritual education is a brute" (*Some Answered Questions* 119). He further observes, "Were there no educator, all souls would remain savage, and were it not for the teacher, the children would be ignorant creatures" (*Selections* 126).

Clearly, however, the teacher can only have an effect when there is a potential for spiritual perfections within the student, and such potentiality is the key to understanding the Bahá'í concept of this vital but subtle relationship between the educator and the student. In one of the most often cited passages on the human condition, Bahá'u'lláh likens human potentiality to a mine rich in gems—the function of the educator is to help discover the treasures in that mine, to bring them into the light and help polish and refine them: "Regard man as a mine rich in gems of inestimable value. Education can, alone, cause it to reveal its treasures, and enable mankind to benefit therefrom" (*Gleanings* 260). 'Abdu'l-Bahá observes the same principle when He states that "education cannot alter the inner essence of a man, but it doth exert a tremendous influence, and with this power it can bring forth from the individual whatever perfections and capacities are deposited within him" (*Selections* 132).

As we have already observed, principal among the educators of man are the Manifestations, Whose every word and action are designed to instruct. And while we will later discuss in detail some of the methods by which they instruct us, we should here note some of the special characteristics that render them especially effective in bringing about human enlightenment.

For one thing, a Manifestation is not merely an enlightened human being; the Manifestation has a power, a capacity, a spiritual essence superior to the station and nature of human beings. Where we as human beings take our beginning when the soul associates with our physical reality at conception, the Manifestation is preexistent. Where we must acquire learning, the Manifestation possesses innate knowledge. Here we are not referring to the revelation itself, a process which begins at a particular point in their lives and which we have come to associate with some outward sign: Moses' seeing the burning bush, Buddha under the Bo tree, Christ's baptism in the Jordan, Muḥammad's visions in the desert, the Báb's vision of the Imám Ḥusayn, Bahá'u'lláh's vision in the Síyáh-Chál. Well before they begin their ministries, even while children, the Manifestations demonstrate that they possess a knowledge that they have not acquired from any earthly source. One and all the Manifestations exhibit exemplary character. In fact, inasmuch as each manifests perfectly the attributes of God, each becomes the expression of God in human form. As we have already noted, this is not to say that they are God or that they are of the same essence as God. As a mirror can reflect the heat and light of the sun without becoming the sun, so the Manifestations demonstrate to us God's nature in dramatic form without becoming God. Therefore, Christ could say to Philip, "He who has seen me has seen the Father" (John 14:9) without in any sense implying that He was God in the flesh. To clarify His point, Christ continues in that same conversation to explain, "The words that I say to you I do not speak on my own authority; but the Father who dwells in me does his works" (John 14:10).

Christ's response also leads us to the focal point of how the Manifestations are utilized by God for our instruction, the process of revelation itself. For while ordinary human beings have the capacity to manifest the attributes of God and even to become divinely inspired, some to a high degree, the Manifestations are uniquely endowed with the mission of becoming a channel through which the word of God is revealed directly to man. 'Abdu'l-Bahá explains this capacity in part when He says that the Manifestations possess a "universal divine mind" which "embraces existing realities" and "receives the light of the mysteries of God" (*Some Answered Questions* 218). 'Abdu'l-Bahá goes on to state that this power is not like our own intellectual power, a product of "investigation and research," but is "a conscious power" unique to the Manifestations:

> The intellectual power of the world of nature is a power of investigation, and by its researches it discovers the realities of beings and the properties of existences; but the heavenly intellectual power, which is beyond nature, embraces things and is cognizant of things, knows them, understands them, is aware of mysteries, realities and divine significations, and is the discoverer of the concealed verities of the Kingdom. This divine intellectual power is the special attribute of the Holy Manifestations and the Dawning-places of prophethood; a ray of this light falls upon the mirrors of the hearts of the righteous, and a portion and a share of this power comes to them through the Holy Manifestations. (*Some Answered Questions* 218)

We may attribute great influence and capacity to certain spiritualized human beings, but powerful as they may be, they operate under the influence of the Manifestations and reflect the light released by their revelations, even though no direct or apparent relationship may be easily detected.

The Manifestations thus have untold influence. It would not be an exaggeration to say that human history is organized around their appearances. And yet each of them forthrightly attributes every action He takes and every word He utters to God acting through Him. For example, according to Scripture God instructed Moses what to do and assured Him that God would provide the words: "And you shall speak to him [Aaron] and put the words in his mouth; and I will be with your mouth and with his mouth, and will teach you what you shall do" (Exod. 4:15). Likewise, in explaining the authority of His words, Christ stated, "For I have not spoken on my own authority; the Father who sent me has himself given me commandment what to say and what to speak" (John 12:49).

In the Qur'án Muḥammad often begins passages with the word *Say* to indicate He is repeating what God has told Him to speak. To explain this process, Muḥammad states in one passage that He cannot adapt or change the Qur'án to accommodate the desires of His followers because He is the channel through which God speaks to them and not the author of the words:

> But when our clear signs are recited to them, they who look not forward to meet Us, say, "Bring a different Koran from this, or make some change in it." Say: It is not for me to change it as mine own soul prompteth. I follow only what is revealed to me. . . . (10:16)

More than twelve hundred years later, in His letter to Muḥammad Sháh, the Báb similarly described the process of revelation:

> God beareth Me witness, I was not a man of learning, for I was trained as a merchant. In the year sixty [1844 A.D.] God graciously infused my soul with the conclusive evidence and weighty knowledge which characterize Him Who is the Testimony of God—may peace be upon Him—until finally in that year I proclaimed God's hidden Cause and unveiled its well-guarded Pillar, in such wise that no one could refute it. (12)

Likewise, Bahá'u'lláh confirms that His revelation is not "of Mine own volition":

> Whenever I chose to hold My peace and be still, lo, the Voice of the Holy Spirit, standing on My right hand, aroused Me, and the Most

Great Spirit appeared before My face, and Gabriel overshadowed Me,
and the Spirit of Glory stirred within My bosom, bidding Me arise and
break My silence. (qtd. in *God Passes By* 102)

Preexistent, aware of each other, fully coordinated in their
actions and words, the Manifestations of God Who perfectly reflect
all the attributes of God educate by degrees the human race, the
fruit of creation in whom "are potentially revealed all the attributes
and names of God" (Bahá'u'lláh, *Kitáb-i-Íqán* 101). Gradually the
Manifestations transform this virtually untapped potentiality into a
reality. And from these primal sources of external instruction derive
other benign teachers who follow their example and advice
—parents, educators, all of those endowed with the noble and
awesome task of guiding humanity.

As we have already observed, a less overt but nonetheless
significant external source of guidance is the physical world itself
with its capacity to reflect the attributes of God. Properly perceived
and understood, the world of nature becomes for us a textbook of
divine instruction: "Within every blade of grass are enshrined the
mysteries of an inscrutable wisdom, and upon every rosebush a
myriad nightingales pour out, in blissful rapture, their melody"
(Bahá'u'lláh, *Kitáb-i-Íqán* 198).

Whether the source of external assistance is the revelation of a
Manifestation or some more indirect instruction such as the inspired
guidance of a parent or teacher, we may conclude that the Bahá'í
paradigm clearly portrays the human being as needing help in order
to achieve the condition of autonomy that we have described as
human fulfillment. Because of this requisite the Bahá'í writings
describe the obligation of the parents and the community to instruct
its children as one of their most fundamental and serious responsibilities. 'Abdu'l-Bahá, for example, states that "no nobler deed than
this can be imagined" (*Selections* 139). The reason for such lofty
praise is explained clearly in numerous passages. 'Abdu'l-Bahá
states that without training the human being is potentially the
source of incalculable iniquity; with it the human spirit is able to
become utterly transcendent: "Every child is potentially the light of
the world—and at the same time its darkness; wherefore must the

question of education be accounted as of primary importance"
(*Selections* 130).

The Internal Mechanism of Justice

In spite of the fact that we are dependent on external influence for
education and progress, the Bahá'í writings make it clear that we
are all largely responsible for our own spiritual advancement. This
condition of freely chosen ascent is virtually a definition of human
justice and an essential ingredient in the Bahá'í paradigm, but it
also may be the most difficult to grasp. That is, we can never know
precisely where external guidance leaves off and our own free
choice begins, but we do know that without our active participation
in the process, human education is impossible. We cannot be
programmed or coerced or brainwashed into true fulfillment, even
if we would like to be.

To understand the basic theory underlying the distinction
between the need for external assistance and the simultaneous
dependence on our own free will, 'Abdu'l-Bahá employs an
effective analogy in which He compares man to a boat. In this
figurative image the force of the wind or steam represents the
external forces which impel the boat into motion, and the boat's
rudder represents individual free will:

> the inaction or the movement of man depend upon the assistance of
> God. If he is not aided, he is not able to do either good or evil. But
> when the help of existence comes from the Generous Lord, he is able
> to do both good and evil; but if the help is cut off, he remains
> absolutely helpless. . . . So this condition is like that of a ship which is
> moved by the power of the wind or steam; if this power ceases, the
> ship cannot move at all. Nevertheless, the rudder of the ship turns it to
> either side, and the power of the steam moves it in the desired
> direction.
>
> In the same way, in all the action or inaction of man, he receives
> power from the help of God; but the choice of good or evil belongs to
> the man himself. (*Some Answered Questions* 249–50)

The awesome significance of our volition 'Abdu'l-Bahá implies when He refers to this power as "a mighty will" (*Promulgation* 178). He states that in spite of the things beyond the control of mankind, the most significant human concerns are "subject to the free will of man, such as justice, equity, tyranny and injustice, in other words, good and evil actions. . . . " (*Some Answered Questions* 248).

We may not always understand exactly when our will is operating independently, but we do know that as a faculty of the human soul, the will is independent of our capacity to feel or to know. For example, we may choose to do that which is contrary to our desires because we realize that some long-term benefit will derive from a short-term discomfort. Likewise, we may understand that our desires are often unreliable guides to proper action. Thus we may be emotionally attracted to something or some course of action and yet choose to ignore such feelings in order to comply with what we consider to be a higher concern, such as compliance with a moral law.

Our will is also clearly a faculty distinct from our ability to know. For example, we may know what is best for us and yet fail to decide on a proper course of action. Or we may intellectually observe that we should follow a certain course of action but ultimately fail to transform that perception into deeds.

There is, in other words, a necessary alliance between free will and action. To exercise our will signifies more than intent—it implies the implementation of intention into a course of action. Thus when we try to determine what is fitting or appropriate for the fulfillment of a human being—what is a just way for an enlightened soul to behave—we come to see that it is the exercise of an entire process: to know and understand, then to determine to implement that understanding in an appropriate dramatic expression, and finally to carry out that intent.

'Abdu'l-Bahá refers to this very process when He states that any accomplishment is achieved through "knowledge, volition and action" (*Promulgation* 157). Similar to the dictates of the Short Obligatory Prayer revealed by Bahá'u'lláh, which ascribes to mankind the purpose of coming "to know Thee and to worship Thee" (*Bahá'í Prayers* 4), 'Abdu'l-Bahá's prescription for human transformation can be found throughout His writings and talks. It is at the heart of His definition of "faith" when He observes that "by faith is meant, first, conscious knowledge, and second, the practice of good deeds" (*Tablets of Abdul-Baha Abbas* 3:549).

Clearly necessary for performing any important deed is conscious choice, just as worship requires a decision or choice followed by action. It is not sufficient that we understand the guidance which the physical sources of education reveal to us. In the Kingdom of Names it is further necessary that we exercise our willpower with enough persistence to manifest our inner transformation with the external signs of noble deeds. No doubt the Apostle James had such willpower in mind when he stated that faith or belief does not exist until it becomes expressed in action:

> What does it profit, my brethren, if a man says he has faith but has not works? Can his faith save him? If a brother or sister is ill-clad and in lack of daily food, and one of you says to them, "Go in peace, be warmed and filled," without giving them the things needed for the body, what does it profit? So faith by itself, if it has no works, is dead. (James 2:14–17)

Reward and Punishment: The Twin Pillars of Justice

Upholding the entire system we have so far delineated is yet another essential ingredient of the Bahá'í theoretical paradigm, the twin "pillars" of reward and punishment. Alluded to throughout the Bahá'í writings as upholding justice in all its forms, this system is a bulwark of the divine structure of creation:

> O people of God! That which traineth the world is Justice, for it is upheld by two pillars, reward and punishment. These two pillars are the sources of life to the world. (Bahá'u'lláh, *Tablets of Bahá'u'lláh* 128–29)

In some passages it is apparent that the system of reward and punishment represents literal institutions which uphold social order by physically restraining the iniquitous:

> Justice hath a mighty force at its command. It is none other than reward and punishment for the deeds of men. By the power of this force the tabernacle of order is established throughout the world, causing the wicked to restrain their natures for fear of punishment. (Bahá'u'lláh, *Tablets of Bahá'u'lláh* 164)

Yet the more deeply we study the relationship of reward and punishment to the physical paradigm, the more we understand its amazing subtlety and pervasiveness.

The purpose of the system of reward and punishment, when it is applied wisely by parents, educators, and the other trainers of mankind, is, according to the Bahá'í teachings, to instigate autonomous motion, not to dominate or oppress. In recent decades, for example, psychologists have observed the benefits of so-called "operant conditioning" in motivating depressed patients or in modifying other behavioral and emotional responses.* Certainly, parents know that it is virtually impossible to train a child without wisely applying reward and punishment on a regular basis. But we have also recently become aware of the danger of misapplying such training. Used too strictly or used oppressively, reward and punishment can destroy autonomy, can produce a mindless fanatic, the exact opposite of what is desired. In short, these twin stimuli are tools of training, not ends in themselves.

The purpose of rewards, punishments, and other trainers is to initiate a response and then to transfer the responsibility for considered action to the individual. This transference is accomplished when the human being becomes enlightened about the rational and benign objectives which the system upholds. When we understand and adopt the goals of human transformation, external guidance through reward and punishment can be lessened or withdrawn because we have internalized the system—we feel

---

*Extending the theories of conditioning set forth by Pavlov and later by B. F. Skinner, modern therapists have come to incorporate systems of reward and punishment to induce specific patterns of behavior, thereby modifying or eliminating an unhealthy response and creating in its place a new conditioned or "operant" response.

good when we succeed and bad when we fail. In short, we train and develop our "conscience" and come to appreciate the relationship between present response and future rewards and punishments.

The same principles of training the conscience are as true for society as they are for the individual. That is, the collective body of mankind has the goal of being in motion toward "an ever-advancing civilization" (Bahá'u'lláh, *Gleanings* 215), and social justice as a system of reward and punishment attempts to train society to achieve that motion. And yet the system of reward and punishment cannot by itself accomplish the goal of spiritual transformation; if society does not comprehend and eventually internalize this goal, reward and punishment will be powerless to enforce order, let alone produce an advancing civilization. Certainly, contemporary attempts at law enforcement and penology confirm this verity. As 'Abdu'l-Bahá notes, effective training cannot be accomplished in a materially oriented system of reward and punishment:

> With force and punishments, material civilization seeketh to restrain the people from mischief, from inflicting harm on society and committing crimes. But in a divine civilization, the individual is so conditioned that with no fear of punishment, he shunneth the perpetration of crimes, seeth the crime itself as the severest of torments, and with alacrity and joy, setteth himself to acquiring the virtues of humankind, to furthering human progress, and to spreading light across the world. (*Selections* 133)

In addition to the wise application of reward and punishment by the educators of mankind, there are at least two other parts of the physical paradigm where we can observe these twin pillars upholding justice. The first is found in our relationship with the natural world. As we have repeatedly observed, there is in the Bahá'í perception of the physical world a belief that the physical world in general and the natural world in particular reflect spiritual attributes, and that this, indeed, is their primary function as an expression of divine will. But Bahá'ís further believe that beyond whatever spiritual qualities physical objects may express on their own is the expression of divine principles in the various relationships among such objects.

The bulk of humanity is only beginning to understand such relationships, as is evidenced most dramatically in our meager awareness of ecology, a dramatic expression of the essential unity of creation. What we are also beginning to understand is that built into the intricate web of relationships among physical objects is the law of reward and punishment. We now see that a violation of nature is not only a travesty against natural beauty and wildlife; it wreaks punishment upon ourselves—we must breathe foul air, eat contaminated food, and drink putrid water. When we fail to appreciate the unity and essentially spiritual nature of the Kingdom of Names, we are punished, and this punishment will force us to reexamine our response to the natural world even if our more overt education does not. So it is that even the strictest materialist ultimately must pay careful attention to the pragmatic exigencies of spiritual relationships within the physical world.

Another less obvious application of the twin pillars of reward and punishment lies in the practical implication of our response to moral law. Traditionally, we think of moral law and social ordinances as deriving from and being upheld by different sources. This type of thinking explains why some politicians consider themselves beyond the constraints of a code of behavior, other than the dictates of practicality or utilitarianism. Likewise, the perpetrator of social injustice, be it an individual criminal or society as a whole, may perceive moral law as irrelevant to its affairs. According to Bahá'í beliefs these perceptions are erroneous. As we have noted, it is the Bahá'í belief that the physical world is, in reality, but the spiritual world expressed in concrete symbols. As such, the relationships among all constituent parts of the physical world are expressions of relationships in the spiritual realm. More to the point, all social law is, when correctly devised, an expression of moral or spiritual law, and as such it is operant whether or not the individual or the society wishes it to be.

Because moral law is always influencing our lives, it has the weight of physical law. If we jump from the top of a three-story building, we do not need to wonder whether the law of gravity will be operant—we know that we will be punished. The same holds true for moral law. If an individual is unjust to others, he will suffer injury to his soul as well as to the success of his mundane enterprises because moral law is not simply a wish or a stricture relevant only to the spiritual realm. It has practical consequences and delineates the most propitious course of action in the physical world.

Nowhere are the consequences of moral laxity more evident than in the study of large-scale social injustice. While a tyrannical social force may endure for a while and seem to succeed by virtue of its own injustice, this same force is inevitably doomed to failure because injustice is impractical inasmuch as it does not comply with reality. Consequently, injustice will produce a negative result, a form of punishment. Take as examples economic systems built on some form of oppression. Such immoral societies are doomed to failure because they assume that humanity is neither equal nor one organic family. Eventually, the error of economic oppression will undermine the most practical affairs of such societies, as is exemplified in the decline of feudalism or of the American plantation in the South, both of which subsisted on slave labor.

We could extend our discussion of the practical implications of moral law to virtually every facet of human endeavor, whether we examine the manufacturing of products or the organizing of the simplest kinds of enterprises. In later chapters we will discuss further the practical relationships of moral law to daily life, but for our purposes here it is sufficient to conclude that the system of reward and punishment which operates throughout the physical world is inherent in the Kingdom of Names itself. Indeed, Bahá'u'lláh may well be alluding to these twin pillars in the Hidden Word which states:

> Out of the wastes of nothingness, with the clay of My command I made thee to appear, and have ordained for thy training every atom in existence and the essence of all created things. Thus, ere thou didst issue from thy mother's womb, I destined for thee two founts of gleaming milk, eyes to watch over thee, and hearts to love thee. (*Hidden Words* 32)

In addition to whatever other meanings they imply, these "founts" may well refer to the twin pillars of reward and punishment as the benign guidance which is infused into every part of the physical world to stimulate autonomy of motion toward human perfection.

Grace and Mercy

In spite of our discussion of the direct and indirect methods by which the physical world is devised to instruct mankind, our outline of the Bahá'í paradigm would be quite incomplete without a final ingredient which functions as a divine elixir to anoint the entire system—that final touch of perfection in God's justice which we call "grace."

It might seem strange to include grace as part of a system of justice since the two terms seem antithetical—the term *justice* usually connotes the exact opposite of *grace*. 'Abdu'l-Bahá acknowledges this antithesis when He states that "bounty is giving without desert, and justice is giving what is deserved" (*Some Answered Questions* 232). Therefore, since we are fallible and, from the standpoint of spiritual development, in a childlike state, if we were to be judged according to strict justice, we would surely be doomed. Bahá'u'lláh confirms as much in the beginning of the Kitáb-i-Íqán, where He describes the supreme irony in the fact that humanity has historically rejected the very Educators sent to give assistance:

> And whensoever the portals of grace did open, and the clouds of divine bounty did rain upon mankind, and the light of the Unseen did shine above the horizon of celestial might, they all denied Him, and turned away from His face—the face of God Himself. Refer ye, to verify this truth, to that which hath been recorded in every sacred Book. (*Kitáb-i-Íqán* 4)

But as we have already observed, the term *justice* in its most ample sense designates propriety, that which is most appropriate and fulfilling of inherent purpose. If we liken mankind at its present stage of development to children, and if we further understand God as being like a loving parent, justice dictates that mercy and grace are appropriate to man. Certainly, a parent's love does not cease because a child has made mistakes, even though the parent may temporarily respond with punishment to guide the wayward child. Similarly, while God is sometimes portrayed in the scriptures of world religions as a strict judge, and while even the Bahá'í writings praise the fear of God as laudable, all world religions teach that God is ever-forgiving and merciful.

Of course, as we have also noted, grace and mercy cannot be imposed against our will. To receive bounty we must desire it and act on that desire. The Báb states in one prayer, "Glorified art Thou, O Lord, Thou forgivest at all times the sins of such among Thy servants as implore Thy pardon" (*Bahá'í Prayers* 82). Thus, when the Báb states in the Qayyúmu'l-Asmá' that "verily God will not forgive disbelief in Himself" (*Selections from the Writings of the Báb* 48), He is not necessarily describing God's retribution so much as He is delineating the relationship between free will and grace: God will not impose forgiveness, and disbelief as a rejection of divine reality implies a refusal of grace. Bahá'u'lláh implies the same thing when He says, "Woe betide him who hath rejected the grace of God and His bounty, and hath denied His tender mercy and authority. . . . " (*Tablets of Bahá'u'lláh* 48).

God's grace and mercy are essential to our success in the physical world because we need many chances if we are to succeed. Fortunately for us, this bounty is always available to us regardless of what we may have done, but it is not automatic. To receive this redeeming mercy, we must follow the same pattern required for every other spiritual effort—knowledge, volition, and action. We must recognize what it is we need and act accordingly by expressing our desire in prayer and in obedience to the guidance of God as revealed to us throughout our association with the Kingdom of Names.

With these nine features of the Bahá'í view of a justly functioning physical creation we have a basic understanding of how physical reality is devised to ensure the appropriate results for which it has been designed and created—an "ever-advancing" civilization on this planet, and an entire organic, universal system, eternal in the past and eternal in the future, in which planets evolve spiritually and contribute to the benign purposes of the whole system. Justice, in this sense, is the propriety of the entire plan of the Creator whereby each atom in creation has a part to play.

And yet, satisfying as this abbreviated sketch of the larger implications of the Bahá'í vision of justice may be, such an analysis is, by itself, hardly a satisfying vision of how we in our daily lives may employ our physical environment for our own advancement. We may be reassured that creation is logically and benignly devised, but we may have no clear sense of how such insight can provide us with practical assistance in accomplishing our just and proper goals of knowing and worshiping God. Obviously, what we now need is to understand how on a daily basis we can work toward spiritual goals through physical activity.

A Guide to the Physical Classroom　　　**3**

Out of the wastes of nothingness, with the clay of My command I made thee to appear, and have ordained for thy training every atom in existence and the essence of all created things.

—Bahá'u'lláh

Having examined the Bahá'í view of physical creation as just and logically devised, we have responded to the first of our three concerns—the theoretical basis for a belief in divine justice. Our second task is to move from theology to practicality—to determine how this theoretically just and appropriate environment assists us on a daily basis to know and to worship God. This objective is perhaps more profound and certainly more immediately satisfying than the first. It would certainly seem to respond more powerfully to the questions raised by Job and Boethius if such a practical analysis could provide insight into how ostensibly negative experience and unjust suffering produce positive results. In short, it is well and good to assert eternal providence and discern a coherent and logical set of laws and principles at work in creation. But a much more satisfying proof of the propriety of physical existence would be the ability to comprehend the methods by which we learn spiritual lessons in a physical classroom.

The Essential Unity of Human Experience

The first step in understanding how to use physical reality is to comprehend in more detail an idea we considered in the previous chapter, that the two sorts of experiences—the physical and the spiritual—and the two realms in which they operate—the physical world and the spiritual world—are but aspects of one coherent and unified experience.

We began our study of physical reality by observing that as humans we have substantially lost a sense of ourselves as unified beings. Even as Bahá'ís we may approach physical experience with trepidation if we infer from some passages in the Bahá'í writings that we should reject the physical world:

> Blind thine eyes, that thou mayest behold My beauty; stop thine ears, that thou mayest hearken unto the sweet melody of My voice; empty thyself of all learning, that thou mayest partake of My knowledge; and sanctify thyself from riches, that thou mayest obtain a lasting share from the ocean of My eternal wealth. (Bahá'u'lláh, *Hidden Words* 25)

Likewise, we may encounter other passages which seem to confirm this rejection of the physical world and to portray the human organism as being composed of two warring factions: "He has the animal side as well as the angelic side, and the aim of an educator is to so train human souls that their angelic aspect may overcome their animal side" ('Abdu'l-Bahá, *Some Answered Questions* 235).

As we have partially understood from our examination of the Bahá'í theory of physical reality, neither view of the world is, taken by itself, sufficient or truly accurate. There is an inextricable relationship between the two aspects of reality because physical creation is an essential part of our spiritual education, and the spiritual enlightenment of mankind is the source of fulfillment for creation. From such a perspective physical reality and our participation in it are detrimental only when we fail to use the experience correctly, when we fail to train our souls so that we have internal justice—each part doing its proper task, as Plato would say. When we let the phenomenal world become an end in itself rather than a means of gaining access to the spiritual reality it reflects, or when we allow our physical or appetitive nature to rule over our judgmental or volitional faculties, we are, indeed, in a state of injustice, confusion, and internal war. In such a state the physical world is detrimental to our success, but it is not the cause—the cause is our own misuse of temporal reality, our failure to understand the essential unity of our experience.

The relationship between the physical world and the spiritual world, then, is at the heart of appreciating and using the physical classroom. Such a relationship, hinted at by a Platonic philosophy and spelled out in detail in the Bahá'í writings, does not simply affirm that it is possible to obtain spiritual benefits from physical experience; rather, the relationship dictates that the animating principle of creation is its reflection of the spiritual world. In this sense the physical world is a means of gaining access to the spiritual world in the same way that a mirror is a vehicle by which light is conveyed:

> Know thou that the Kingdom is the real world, and this nether place is only its shadow stretching out. A shadow hath no life of its own; its existence is only a fantasy, and nothing more; it is but images reflected in water, and seeming as pictures to the eye. ('Abdu'l-Bahá, *Selections* 178)

This does not imply that the physical world is negative or evil. Properly understood and utilized, physical reality is a means of spiritual ascent, a way to salvation. It is detrimental only when we perceive it as the object of our pilgrimage instead of our means of transportation.

Hence we can appreciate that one of the principal and most difficult tasks of the Manifestations of God is to clarify the essential relationship between the two aspects of our experience—to show us how to use one world to understand the other, how to achieve unity and harmony in our lives and identities as human beings. To help relate one aspect of ourselves to the other, the Manifestation works in two capacities.

As He reiterates the eternal, changeless attributes of the spiritual world, He is a revealer, an unveiler of divine reality and moral law. Accordingly, religious law as it is revealed by the Prophets is not simply an attempt to impose order on disorder. Properly understood, moral or spiritual law assumes the same objective authority as scientific law. As scientific law describes predictable relationships among phenomena, so spiritual or moral law describes predictable relationships among spiritual entities. The laws of the Manifestations are, therefore, descriptive as well as prescriptive. We praise Newton for having discovered and formulated the mutual attraction of masses—the law of gravity—not for having contrived or invented this property of matter. Similarly, the Manifestation does not create divine reality or the laws governing that reality. He reveals them to us and invites compliance with them. Likewise, as advances in scientific understanding render more and more complete our descriptions of the phenomenal world, so the progression of revelation by the successive Manifestations makes our understanding of spiritual reality and spiritual laws more complete and more accurate.

But the Manifestation is not only a describer or revealer. He also makes things happen. In His station as lawgiver He actively affects the degree to which the physical world reflects the spiritual world. He is a creative force Who puts in motion the energies and laws which will cause spiritual reality to become actuated in the phenomenal world. Consequently, when the Manifestation instructs us how to implement spiritual law, He is doing at least two things. He is describing the spiritual principles which underlie and are the logical bases for His social ordinances, and He is establishing the Kingdom of God on earth by implementing those principles in a way consonant with our increased level of human understanding and with our increased capacity for action.

For example, when Bahá'u'lláh institutes the concept of the equality of men and women, He is revealing a spiritual verity which has always existed, and He is pronouncing to what extent the physical world can now implement and reflect that reality. Likewise, when Bahá'u'lláh speaks of the unity of science and religion, He is revealing an objective reality by pointing out that both areas of investigation are probing aspects of one creation. At the same time He admonishes scientists and religious thinkers to become aware of the unity of science and religion so that they can put aside their differences and work together to increase our understanding of existence.

At the heart of the dual function of the Manifestation, then, is the key to the essential union of the physical and spiritual world. By demonstrating to us the harmony of the two worlds, the Manifestation enables us to live successfully in both of them. In fact, if we follow the guidelines provided by the Manifestation for the proper utilization of our physical classroom, we will find that the dedicated study of one reality will inevitably facilitate an understanding of the other. And, as we noted at the outset of this study, the faculties traditionally regarded as specialized for the pursuit of these concerns (the standards of science for the phenomenal world and of faith for the spiritual world) are equally involved in the investigation of both realms.

The Metaphorical Nature of Physical Reality

If we can accept that the physical and spiritual realms, and, consequently, our participation in them, are inextricably related, we can understand the importance of appreciating how each of these seemingly separate and discordant realities is related to the other in the physical world. We can also start to appreciate the wisdom of setting out on our spiritual pilgrimage in physical clothes and can begin to discern exactly how our education takes place.

Perhaps the clearest statement in the Bahá'í writings about the logical basis for such a system of education is found in a passage by 'Abdu'l-Bahá:

> The wisdom of the appearance of the spirit in the body is this: the human spirit is a Divine Trust, and it must traverse all conditions, for its passage and movement through the conditions of existence will be the means of its acquiring perfections. So when a man travels and passes through different regions and numerous countries with system and method, it is certainly a means of his acquiring perfection, for he will see places, scenes and countries, from which he will discover the conditions and states of other nations. . . . It is the same when the human spirit passes through the conditions of existence: it will become the possessor of each degree and station. (*Some Answered Questions* 200)

But what is the "system and method" with which we should approach our journey? What is the specific means by which we relate our physical lives to our spiritual evolution? The means by which the physical world, this nether world of cave and shadow, is related to the spiritual world is the metaphorical process, and in order to understand it, we must appreciate how metaphors work.

A metaphor is one of several kinds of analogical devices, all of which function in the same manner; they compare two essentially dissimilar things (people, situations, relationships, abstractions, material objects, and so on). Always in the comparison is an implicit or explicit statement of similarity between these essentially different subjects. But regardless of whether the analogical device is a metaphor, a simile, an allegory, a conceit, a symbol, or some other type of figure or trope, it contains three basic parts: the *tenor,* that which is being described; the *vehicle,* that which is compared to the tenor; and the *meaning,* that area of similarity between the tenor and the vehicle.*

The term *metaphor* is often used to designate the metaphorical process in general, though strictly speaking, a metaphor is a relatively short, implicit analogical device. Sometimes the terms *figure* or *image* are also used in this general sense, *figure* denoting "figure of speech" or "rhetorical device," and *image* designating "figurative image." But whatever term one uses, and regardless of whether the device is a one-word metaphor or an elaborate parable or allegory, a particularly challenging process must occur if the device is to work effectively. One must be made to think, to be creative, to complete the final and most important part of the process by determining in what way the tenor and vehicle are similar.

Consider the simple metaphor "Jane is a lovely flower." The analogical equation is established because the tenor "Jane" is essentially different from the vehicle "flower." (Had we compared Jane to Mary, the tenor and the vehicle would be essentially the same—both being girls—and no analogy would occur.) The

---

*The terms *tenor* and *vehicle* were coined by I. A. Richards in *The Philosophy of Rhetoric* (London: Oxford Univ. Press, 1936), just one of his numerous studies on metaphor and language.

reader must now finish the equation by deciding what the tenor (Jane) has in common with the vehicle (the flower). Or, to approach the equation from another angle, the reader must decide what the missing link is between the two different objects—the x-factor, the common bond that becomes the meaning for the comparison. If the metaphor is obvious or trite, our thoughts go directly from tenor to meaning without examining the vehicle, without needing to solve the equation for x. Consequently, overworked similes such as "cold as ice" or "hard as stone" require no mental examination of the equation because the vehicle offers no resistance; the process is short-circuited. Description has occurred, but the device has not challenged us to participate in the process of creating a mental image by contributing something of our own.

The value of the metaphorical process is immense, for it is a useful way to explain the unfamiliar in terms of the familiar, or the abstract in terms of the concrete. It also has the capacity to compress a great deal of meaning into few words. Moreover, because it offers a variety of meanings, it can become an expansive description rather than a limiting or restrictive one. But probably the most important feature of the metaphorical process is its ability to educate because when we are forced to examine a vehicle to understand a tenor, we must exercise one of our most important capacities, our faculty of judgment and discernment:

> Metaphor is a process of comparing and identifying one thing with another. Then, as we see what things have in common, we see the general meaning they have. Now, the ability to see the relation between one thing and another is almost a definition of intelligence. Thinking in metaphors . . . is a tool of intelligence. Perhaps it is the most important tool. (Simpson 6)

In addition to exercising our faculty of discernment, we are also extracting the meaning for ourselves instead of having the meaning imposed on us. Therefore, the metaphorical process is indirect and objective in that the teacher who employs it is a step removed from the analogical teaching device. In effect, if we as students are to obtain meaning, we must exercise our volition and examine the tenor and the vehicle for ourselves. When we apprehend the meaning on our own, we will not feel as if we have been told what to think, though we may be grateful to the one who has been creative enough to conceive the equation which led us to a new and richer understanding.

We can hardly discuss the use of the metaphorical process as it relates to religion without mentioning one more vital asset of the device. It is a safeguard against literalism and hence against imitation and dogmatism. For example, when Christ states that He is the "bread of life" (John 6:35), He means something positive by it, that He is valuable, essential, a source of sustenance, of spiritual nutrition. But there is no one "correct" meaning or translation of the equation. Unless we realize that Christ's statement is metaphorical, we may end up believing that Christ was a piece of bread.

Perhaps the most important value of the metaphorical process is its function in human development. Without it man would not be able to transcend the physical world, even for a moment, because in this life abstract thought is impossible without the use of analogy. In order to discuss or comprehend spiritual qualities, we must first relate ephemeral realities to concrete forms. This essential need for using the analogical process to understand abstraction is expressed by 'Abdu'l-Bahá when He explains that

> human knowledge is of two kinds. One is the knowledge of things perceptible to the senses. . . .
> The other kind of human knowledge is intellectual—that is to say, it is a reality of the intellect; it has no outward form and no place and is not perceptible to the senses. . . . Therefore, to explain the reality of the spirit—its condition, its station—one is obliged to give explanations under the forms of sensible things because in the external world all that exists is sensible. For example, grief and happiness are intellectual things; when you wish to express those spiritual qualities you say: "My heart is oppressed; my heart is dilated," though the heart of man is neither oppressed nor dilated. This is an intellectual or spiritual state, to explain which you are obliged to have recourse to sensible figures. Another example: you say, "such an individual made great progress," though he is remaining in the same place; or again, "such a one's position was exalted," although, like everyone else, he walks upon the earth. This exaltation and this progress are spiritual states and intellectual realities, but to explain them you are obliged to

have recourse to sensible figures because in the exterior world there is nothing that is not sensible.

So the symbol of knowledge is light, and of ignorance, darkness; but reflect, is knowledge sensible light, or ignorance sensible darkness? No, they are merely symbols. (*Some Answered Questions* 83–84)

It is the metaphorical process, together with the faculty for inductive logic, which enables us to pass beyond the Pavlovian, or Skinnerian reflex, and to form concepts of ourselves and the world around us. Of course, the process is not confined to educated adults. Wittingly and unwittingly a child collects data from daily experiences, perceives the similarities among experiences, and from the data induces abstract beliefs. For example, when a child is punished or corrected for essentially different actions, he or she, at some point, perceives the common link among the different experiences, the x-factor, perhaps the similar ingredients of rules, or the concept of authority or obedience. The child then induces further generalizations about the concepts and may even perceive that there are rules which require obedience to authority. If the rules at some point prove helpful to his or her well-being, the child may further conclude that authority is worthy of respect and obedience. If there is no consistency to the rules or their administration, the child may induce that authority is capricious, unjust, frightening, and unworthy of respect. The child may not be aware that this process is taking place, that he or she is thinking metaphorically and forming generalizations from the data collected. But the child is constantly doing it all the same.

From the initial stages of abstract thought a child progresses without limit to more encompassing abstractions, since concepts are always in a relative state of being perceived. Once having observed authority dramatized in a familial relationship, for example, a child may later collect and store other dramatizations of this abstraction, perhaps from observations of a teacher or public official. As the process continues, the child continues to collect the data and may perceive authority as a quality beyond what he or she sees embodied in specific people. A belief in truth, honesty, or kindness may represent authority far more powerfully than any human figure. Even in such instances the child is still relating the abstraction to the physical world; he or she has come to understand honesty or kindness as manifested in the physical classroom. But there is no point at which the lesson is completed. The abstraction can always be more acutely perceived, more expansively understood, more exquisitely dramatized in the physical world. And, as we have already observed, such limitless growth is not confined to the individual. Society itself can grow to understand and apply more fully abstract concepts, such as authority, justice, or honesty, and as that collective awareness progresses, the society can become capable of implementing more completely such concepts in social action.

Viewed in the context of our ever-expanding understandings of abstract concepts, the metaphorical process is an educational tool which can help provide unlimited development, even if we have no precise moral code or established theological belief. However, within the context of the Bahá'í perception of man's nature and destiny, this process assumes a much greater significance—not only does this endeavor bring immediate fulfillment and happiness by utilizing the physical metaphor as it was created to be used; it also results in the gradual improvement of the soul itself as, incrementally, particular attributes are habituated and assimilated.

Metaphor and Spiritual Education

The improvement of the soul through the metaphorical dramatization of spiritual attributes is hardly a new idea. The allegorical fable has long been recognized as an effective teaching device. In the medieval era the Christian Church used allegorical theater (morality plays) to teach an unlearned and predominantly illiterate populace the essential doctrines of their faith. In fact, virtually all drama, including classical tragedy, comes from religious origins and the attempt to give tropological expression to metaphysical concepts —to express spirituality in concrete form.

The fact that allegorical storytelling and drama have a long and widespread history does not imply that all metaphorical devices function exactly the same. But all do share essentially the same ingredients and occur according to a similar pattern. First, we come to understand the nature of an attribute or abstract quality by observing how it is dramatized in physical action. Second, we decide to acquire the attribute by resolving to dramatize it in a similar kind of action of our own. Third, we fulfill our noble intent, not once but consistently, repeatedly until the response becomes habitual and instinctive. When a particular attribute has in some degree become habitual, our soul itself can be said to have become changed and improved by the assimilation of the attribute.

But we are not finished. We can now perceive the same attribute as it is reflected in more elaborate, more inclusive forms and then attempt to implement our increased understanding by using the same basic sequence of responses. In this manner our souls continue to progress without ever reaching a final stage of growth since each attribute is infinitely perfectible and since the number of attributes themselves is endless: "When man reaches the noblest state in the world of humanity, then he can make further progress in the conditions of perfection, but not in state; for such states are limited, but the divine perfections are endless" ('Abdu'l-Bahá, *Some Answered Questions* 237).

Physical reality thus functions metaphorically during our earthly lives as an integral and inextricable part of our efforts to achieve spiritual development by providing both the means whereby we perceive the spiritual attributes in the first place and the tools with which we can express and acquire attributes once they are understood. Even as we grow spiritually and are able to respond to increasingly higher levels of understanding, we never relinquish in our physical existence the need to relate that understanding to other instructive metaphors. The reciprocal relationship between knowing and doing remains.

Consider the attribute of cleanliness. A child may first understand this abstraction in terms of seeing the similarity among the diverse acts of cleanliness he or she is required to perform —cleaning play areas, bathing, wearing clean clothes. At the outset these acts are perceived as separate commands, each of which requires understanding, volition, and action. In time each separate act may become habitual. At some point the child will, one hopes, perceive the metaphorical relationship uniting these diverse acts and, instead of having to learn so many specific regulations, be able to reverse the process, to apply an understanding of the quality of cleanliness to other seemingly unrelated physical acts, and, finally, to habituate an expanded awareness of the quality. As the child manifests progressive levels of understanding through habit and discipline, he or she becomes liberated. Gradually the child no longer has to struggle against inertia but is able to perceive even more sophisticated levels of meaning—cleanliness of thought, purity of motive, chastity of conduct, and an infinite variety of other possibilities—each of which will in turn require increased measures of will.

Even a brief treatment of how a child learns cleanliness makes apparent several important features about spiritual growth through the metaphorical process. First, spiritual growth, especially after basic habits are formed, is gradual, painstaking, difficult. There are, no doubt, moments of great insight, visions of great change, possibly days and weeks of rapid advancement. But the enduring and effective change of the human soul is attained slowly, meticulously, wittingly, methodically. Second, habit and discipline, instead of being restrictive or limiting, are, when applied positively to the early formation of attributes, agents of liberation and advancement. It is virtually axiomatic that without some capacity for self-discipline, one cannot be released from one level of response in order to ascend to the next. Consequently, the early training of the child in the formation of good habits and in the initiation of self-discipline is, when properly taught, a key to his or her freedom, a gift and a profound expression of love, not a stifling of the creative spirit. Once accustomed to the rewards of applied habit and discipline, the child will less likely be overwhelmed by the initial difficulties which inevitably occur in the struggle against the natural resistance to growth.

As we will discuss in the section of this chapter entitled "The Metaphorical Lessons in Negative Experience," looking for spiritual growth without discomfort is like trying to become physically conditioned without being willing to endure sore muscles and days of repetitious exercises. If a child has not been trained to persist in spite of anxiety and discomfort, if he or she has not experienced analogous situations where efforts have proved rewarding, the abstract assurance of spiritual rewards will probably not prove sufficient impetus to ensure success. Indeed, nothing is more frustrating or cruel than to admonish a child to be good without helping him or her comprehend what goodness means and how it is acquired.

Being thus aware of the initial discomfort of human growth is particularly important when a child begins to weigh the value of moral principles against the enticements of sensuality. If the child pursues only that which "feels good," he or she is doomed. The same principle holds true in the investigation of religion itself. If we search for a set of beliefs that does not challenge us, if our sole criterion for a religion is that it feel comfortable, we may be in danger of assuming that our current state of development is the standard by which to judge beliefs. Obviously the reverse should be the case—we need to assess our own progress by a standard which is independent of our own condition, a standard based on spiritual truths that continually exhort us to strive beyond our present state of accomplishment.

In the end we may choose not to use the metaphorical classroom to advance our growth, but all creation from the smallest seed to the universe itself exhorts us to fulfill our inherent destiny, to ascend from mere physical subsistence, to soar in the heights of human perfection:

> Thus the embryo of man in the womb of the mother gradually grows and develops, and appears in different forms and conditions, until in the degree of perfect beauty it reaches maturity and appears in a perfect form with the utmost grace. And in the same way, the seed of this flower which you see was in the beginning an insignificant thing, and very small; and it grew and developed in the womb of the earth and, after appearing in various forms, came forth in this condition with perfect freshness and grace. In the same manner, it is evident that this terrestrial globe, having once found existence, grew and developed in the matrix of the universe, and came forth in different forms and conditions, until gradually it attained this present perfection, and

became adorned with innumerable beings, and appeared as a finished organization. ('Abdu'l-Bahá, *Some Answered Questions* 182–83)

Metaphor in the Teaching Techniques of the Manifestations

Since the metaphorical process is the principal means by which spiritual growth is achieved in the physical world, it would seem logical that the process would be evident in the methods of the Manifestations of God, for they are perfect teachers sent to direct man's spiritual development. In other words, it is reasonable to assume that we can discover this process at work in their teaching methods and can further discern how they encourage our utilization of the metaphorical process in carrying out their guidance for our lives. That is precisely what we do find. Metaphorical devices constitute the core of the methodology employed by the Manifestations, and the metaphorical process as a teaching technique is apparent in their actions, language, and laws.

The actions, even the identity of each Manifestation, involve the metaphorical process because, in addition to being an Emissary, the Manifestation is also an Exemplar, a perfect reflection of the attributes of God in motion, a station which relates directly to humanity's twofold purpose: "The purpose of God in creating man hath been, and will ever be, to enable him to know his Creator and to attain His Presence" (Bahá'u'lláh, *Gleanings* 70). Since the Bahá'í writings depict God as essentially unknowable, the most effective means of knowing God is by knowing the Manifestations Who reflect God's essence for us. It is clear that attaining the presence of God does not imply attaining physical proximity but rather changing the spiritual condition of our souls so that we are constantly increasing our capacity for acquiring the spiritual attributes of God, for becoming more like Him (*Gleanings* 184). Yet, as we have already seen, acquisition cannot take place without understanding. In effect, knowing God and attaining His presence are aspects of one process. In this regard Bahá'u'lláh points out in the Kitáb-i-Aqdas that we cannot sever the recognition of the

Manifestation from obedience to His laws: "These twin duties are inseparable. Neither is acceptable without the other" (*Synopsis* 11).

Recognition of the Manifestation is, therefore, a necessary prerequisite for spiritual advancement; it is not sufficient simply to follow a pattern of behavior. Furthermore, recognition of the Manifestation implies more than perceiving the validity of His description of the universe and the pragmatic value of His ordinances or even the value of His sacrificial life. It involves perceiving the way in which the Manifestation metaphorizes or dramatizes God for us. In this way the Manifestation is clearly distinct from all other spiritual teachers, no matter how astute their teachings or how wise their laws. To know God is to know the Manifestation, and to know the Manifestation is to understand the way in which He manifests the qualities of God. In responding to Philip's request to see the Father, about Whom Jesus had said so much during His ministry, Christ states: "'Have I been with you so long, and yet you do not know me, Philip? He who has seen me has seen the Father; how can you say, "Show us the Father"?'" (John 14:9).

In considering Christ's response to Philip, it is crucial, as it is with all metaphors, not to confuse the tenor with the vehicle, not to take the metaphor at its literal value but, rather, to extract the meaning by discerning the similarity between the two components, in this case between Christ (the vehicle) and God (the tenor). Clearly the similarity between these essentially different entities is not physical, since the Manifestation is not necessarily physically impressive and since God is not a physical being. Neither is the similarity in physical power, since none of the Manifestations aspires to earthly ascendancy. The commonly held qualities are spiritual powers and capacities. To confuse the literal or physical nature of the vehicle (the person or personality of the Manifestation) with the tenor He represents (the nature of God) is to do more than misuse an analogy. To miss the metaphorical nature of the relationship between the Manifestation and God is to misunderstand completely the nature of the Manifestation, to fail to understand God Himself, and to confuse the whole educative process by which the Manifestation is attempting to instruct us.

No doubt it is because of the confusion of the vehicle with the tenor that the Manifestations expend so much effort to make clear the metaphorical relationships. For example, even though Christ states that no one can understand God except by first understanding Christ, He explains that He is essentially different from God: "'I am the true vine, and my Father is the vinedresser'" (John 15:1). Furthermore, throughout His teachings He explains that He is not the ultimate source of authority behind the revelation, but a reflection of the Deity Who is:

> "He who believes in me, believes not in me but in him who sent me." (John 12:44)

> "For I have not spoken on my own authority; the Father who sent me has himself given me commandment what to say and what to speak." (John 12:49)

> "The words that I say to you I do not speak on my own authority; but the Father who dwells in me does his works." (John 14:10)

In a similar manner, Bahá'u'lláh explains the relationship of the Manifestation to God and repeatedly enunciates the same theme: He is a tool which God uses to educate men:

> This thing is not from Me, but from One Who is Almighty and All-Knowing. And He bade Me lift up My voice between earth and heaven. . . . (*Epistle* 11)

> This is but a leaf which the winds of the will of thy Lord, the Almighty, the All-Praised, have stirred. (*Epistle* 11–12)

> By My Life! Not of Mine own volition have I revealed Myself, but God, of His own choosing, hath manifested Me. (qtd. in Shoghi Effendi, *God Passes By* 102)

One example of the disastrous results of not recognizing the metaphorical process at work in the nature of the Manifestations is evident in the far-reaching effects of the vote taken at the Council of

Nicaea in 325 A.D. The followers of Athanasius, an Egyptian theologian and ecclesiastical statesman, had come to believe that the tenor and the vehicle were one—that Christ and God were the same essence. The followers of Arius, a Christian priest of Alexandria, believed Christ was essentially inferior to God. A ballot was cast, and Arius lost. The institution of the Church sanctioned the theology of Athanasius, condemned as heresy the views of Arius, and effectively severed itself from Christ's fundamental teaching for all time. As Muḥammad pointed out to the Christians three hundred years later, to equate Christ with God is to add gods to God—in effect, to believe in more than one God as did the idolators of Muḥammad's day:

> Infidels now are they who say, "God is the Messiah, Son of Mary;" for the Messiah said, "O children of Israel! worship God, my Lord and your Lord." Whoever shall join other gods with God, God shall forbid him the Garden, and his abode shall be the Fire; and the wicked shall have no helpers. (Qur'án 5:76)

The use of metaphor is also the key to unlocking the meaning of the physical acts of the Manifestations. Since none of the Manifestations aspires to physical authority or dominion, any expression of physical power by them clearly has limited importance. In healing the sick Christ was not attempting to rid the nation of disease or demonstrate an innovative medical technique. 'Abdu'l-Bahá explains that the miraculous acts of the Manifestations had as their primary purpose the metaphorical or analogical dramatization of a spiritual truth:

> The outward miracles have no importance for the people of Reality. If a blind man receive sight, for example, he will finally again become sightless, for he will die and be deprived of all his senses and powers. Therefore, causing the blind man to see is comparatively of little importance, for this faculty of sight will at last disappear. If the body of a dead person be resuscitated, of what use is it since the body will die again? But it is important to give perception and eternal life—that is, the spiritual and divine life. . . .
> . . . Wherever in the Holy Books they speak of raising the dead, the meaning is that the dead were blessed by eternal life; where it is

said that the blind received sight, the signification is that he obtained the true perception. . . . This is ascertained from the text of the Gospel where Christ said: "These are like those of whom Isaiah said, They have eyes and see not, they have ears and hear not; and I healed them."

The meaning is not that the Manifestations are unable to perform miracles, for They have all power. But for Them inner sight, spiritual healing and eternal life are the valuable and important things. (*Some Answered Questions* 101–02)

It is with obvious wisdom, therefore, that Bahá'u'lláh and 'Abdu'l-Bahá exhort Bahá'ís not to place any emphasis on the miracles associated with Bahá'u'lláh. As 'Abdu'l-Bahá points out, the act is valuable only to those who witness the event, and even those may doubt what they have seen:

I do not wish to mention the miracles of Bahá'u'lláh, for it may perhaps be said that these are traditions, liable both to truth and to error. . . . Though if I wish to mention the supernatural acts of Bahá'u'lláh, they are numerous; they are acknowledged in the Orient, and even by some non-Bahá'ís. . . . Yes, miracles are proofs for the eyewitness only, and even he may regard them not as a miracle but as an enchantment. (*Some Answered Questions* 37)

There is also an obvious temptation on the part of the followers of a Manifestation to praise Him for physical miracles and to perceive Him as a figure of temporal power instead of spiritual authority. It is understandably easier for the followers to become attracted to the vehicle, the personalities of the Manifestations themselves and the literal acts they perform, than to recognize the similarity between these Vehicles and the spiritual forces and attributes they metaphorize for us.

One of the clearest examples of such a mistaken perception, besides the almost inevitable attachment to the physical person of the Manifestation, is the incident of Christ's feeding of the five thousand. After He performed the miracle of feeding the masses with only five barley loaves and two fishes, the people believed Him to be a Prophet. When Christ saw that they wanted to take Him by force and make Him king, He fled to the hills. He explained the reason for His action to His disciples the next day when they found Him on the opposite side of the Sea of Galilee:

> "Truly, truly, I say to you, you seek me, not because you saw signs, but because you ate your fill of the loaves. Do not labor for the food which perishes, but for the food which endures to eternal life, which the Son of man will give to you; for on him has God the Father set his seal." (John 6:26–27)

When the people failed to understand the metaphorical meaning or inner significance of His act and wanted to follow Him for the phenomenal value of the physical event, He left them. The importance He placed on their grasping the inner significance of His actions is further evident in the patience with which He continued His explanation:

> "Our fathers ate the manna in the wilderness; as it is written, 'He gave them bread from heaven to eat.'" Jesus then said to them, "Truly, truly, I say to you, it was not Moses who gave you the bread from heaven; my Father gives you the true bread from heaven. For the bread of God is that which comes down from heaven, and gives life to the world." They said to him, "Lord, give us this bread always."
>
> Jesus said to them, "I am the bread of life; he who comes to me shall not hunger, and he who believes in me shall never thirst." (John 6:31–35)

If we think that Christ belabored the imagery of the bread from heaven, we are wrong. Even when He repeated and extended the conceit, the Jews did not appreciate the metaphorical intent of His actions or of His words as He continued to explain:

> "I am the living bread which came down from heaven; if any one eats of this bread, he will live for ever; and the bread which I shall give for the life of the world is my flesh."
>
> The Jews then disputed among themselves, saying, "How can this man give us his flesh to eat?" (John 6:51–52)

Having been raised in a legalistic religious tradition, the Jews had difficulty understanding teachings which were communicated through metaphor, even though most of their own ritual originally was symbolic or metaphorical dramatization. In a very real sense the actions and teaching methods of Christ were aimed at breaking through their literalism, at teaching them to think metaphorically, to sense the spirit behind the outer form of religion. As one of His last actions among His disciples, for example, He continued the bread imagery at the Last Supper:

> Now as they were eating, Jesus took bread, and blessed, and broke it, and gave it to the disciples and said, "Take, eat; this is my body." And he took a cup, and when he had given thanks he gave it to them, saying, "Drink of it, all of you; for this is my blood of the covenant, which is poured out for many for the forgiveness of sins." (Matt. 26:26–28)

In this case, a verbal metaphor was not sufficient; Christ had His own disciples act out the metaphor.

The life of Bahá'u'lláh also contains many actions with obvious metaphorical value. The conference at Badasht is perhaps one of the most intriguing. The purpose of the occasion was, according to Shoghi Effendi, to "implement the revelation of the Bayán by a sudden, a complete and dramatic break with the past—with its order, its ecclesiasticism, its traditions, and ceremonials" (*God Passes By* 31). In order to act out this transition metaphorically Bahá'u'lláh rented three gardens, one for Himself, one for Quddús, a third for Ṭáhirih. According to a prearranged plan Quddús and Ṭáhirih publicly quarreled during the conference, Quddús advocating a conservative view that the followers of the Báb not dissociate themselves from the religion of Islam, and Ṭáhirih urging a complete break with Islam:

> It was Bahá'u'lláh Who steadily, unerringly, yet unsuspectedly, steered the course of that memorable episode, and it was Bahá'u'lláh Who brought the meeting to its final and dramatic climax. One day in His presence, when illness had confined Him to bed, Ṭáhirih, regarded as the fair and spotless emblem of chastity and the incarnation of the holy Fáṭimih, appeared suddenly, adorned yet unveiled, before the assembled companions, seated herself on the right hand of the affrighted and infuriated Quddús, and, tearing through her fiery

words the veils guarding the sanctity of the ordinances of Islám, sounded the clarion-call, and proclaimed the inauguration, of a new Dispensation. (*God Passes By* 32)*

This dramatic event no doubt had many metaphorical meanings, not the least of which was a transition from one "garden" (Islam) to a completely new "garden" (the Bábí revelation). We may also find symbolic value in the fact that Bahá'u'lláh occupied a third "garden," possibly a symbol of His own revelation, in the same way that one of the Hidden Words employs a garden image to represent the new revelation:

> Proclaim unto the children of assurance that within the realms of holiness, nigh unto the celestial paradise, a new garden hath appeared, round which circle the denizens of the realm on high and the immortal dwellers of the exalted paradise. (Bahá'u'lláh, *Hidden Words* 27)

Not all the actions of the Manifestations and their followers are so clearly symbolic or metaphorical, though one can hardly ignore the overall dramatic and metaphorical tenor of the entire Heroic Age of the Bahá'í Faith. But, strictly speaking, all the actions of the Manifestation have the capacity to express God's love for man through dramatic physical action.

Possibly the most obvious use of metaphor as a teaching device by the Manifestations is in the language they use. Whether it is the allegorical myths of the Old Testament, the parables of Christ, or the exquisite poetic imagery of Bahá'u'lláh's verses, the language of the Manifestations frequently relies on figures drawn from the phenomenal world in order to translate abstract concepts into terms which men can more readily understand. To render a comparative analysis of the types of imagery used by the successive Manifestations would require countless volumes, but several general observations

---

*See also Nabíl-i-A'zam [Muhammad-i-Zarandí], *The Dawn-Breakers: Nabíl's Narrative of the Early Days of the Bahá'í Revelation*, trans. and ed. Shoghi Effendi (Wilmette, Ill.: Bahá'í Publishing Trust, 1932), p. 294, n. 1.

will be sufficient for our purposes to demonstrate how essential metaphor is in the language of these Teachers.

As Bahá'u'lláh explains in the Kitáb-i-Íqán, the Manifestations do not always use language which is veiled, allusive, metaphorical; the way they speak depends on the exigencies of the situation:

> It is evident unto thee that the Birds of Heaven and Doves of Eternity speak a twofold language. One language, the outward language, is devoid of allusions, is unconcealed and unveiled; that it may be a guiding lamp and a beaconing light whereby wayfarers may attain the heights of holiness, and seekers may advance into the realm of eternal reunion. Such are the unveiled traditions and the evident verses already mentioned. The other language is veiled and concealed, so that whatever lieth hidden in the heart of the malevolent may be made manifest and their innermost being be disclosed. . . . In such utterances, the literal meaning, as generally understood by the people, is not what hath been intended. (*Kitáb-i-Íqán* 254–55)

An illustration of Bahá'u'lláh's statement might be the distinction we would make between the language with which the Manifestation reveals His laws and the language with which He inspires and explains spiritual attributes.

There are no exact rules about when a Manifestation will speak metaphorically and when He will not. As we study the Old Testament, we can only guess how literally the followers of Abraham or Moses perceived the anthropomorphic descriptions of God and the physical evidences of His intervention in the lives of men. But two major uses of metaphorical language seem relatively consistent, at least with Christ and Bahá'u'lláh.

One recurring use is in portraying concepts of spirituality, for which purpose Christ employed the parable. Like other metaphorical devices, the parable forces the listener to participate, to decide the meaning; but being an extended analogy in the form of a story, the parable has the further advantage of working on various levels with multiple metaphoric equations, and of holding the listener's interest, since it is also a dramatic narrative. Thus while Christ was establishing an intimacy with the literal story by using characters and situations familiar to His audience (a prodigal son, laborers in a vineyard, sowers of seed), He was also teaching His followers to think abstractly, to escape the literalism of their inherited beliefs, and to understand the spiritual or inner significance of His words. Instead of an elaborate canon of law (though He did leave laws as well), He gave His believers a treasury of memorable stories, each one of which had the capacity to operate on a variety of levels. Any seeker, the highest or the lowest, the learned as well as the untutored, could appreciate Christ's parables in a different way. But those entrapped in their literalism could not penetrate the metaphorical lessons, neither could they grasp the figurative implications of their own Messianic prophecies:

> Then the disciples came and said to him, "Why do you speak to them in parables?" And he answered them, "To you it has been given to know the secrets of the kingdom of heaven, but to them it has not been given. For to him who has will more be given, and he will have abundance; but from him who has not, even what he has will be taken away. This is why I speak to them in parables, because seeing they do not see, and hearing they do not hear, nor do they understand." (Matt. 13:10–13)

Christ later told His disciples that "the hour is coming when I shall no longer speak to you in figures but tell you plainly of the Father" (John 16:25). Certainly Bahá'u'lláh fulfills this promise with the revelation of the Kitáb-i-Íqán. In this volume Bahá'u'lláh explains forthrightly God's divine plan, describes the nature of the Manifestations, and clarifies the logical basis for their teaching methods.

Yet Bahá'u'lláh does use imagery magnificently when it is needed. In His meditative writings, in most of His prayers, in the second half of the Hidden Words, and in various other poetic and allusive tablets Bahá'u'lláh has bequeathed a storehouse of figurative imagery and symbolism. In fact, in describing those utterances in which "the literal meaning, as generally understood by the people, is not what hath been intended," Bahá'u'lláh states:

> Thus it is recorded: "Every knowledge hath seventy meanings, of which one only is known amongst the people. And when the Qá'im

shall arise, He shall reveal unto men all that which remaineth." He also saith: "We speak one word, and by it we intend one and seventy meanings; each one of these meanings we can explain." (*Kitáb-i-Íqán* 255)

Of course, the fact that the Manifestation can explain all the meanings does not mean He will. Like Christ with His parables, Bahá'u'lláh most often does not explicate His own imagery but tests our sincerity by forcing us to extract for ourselves the inner essence of His teachings. Obviously it would be pretentious and, for our purposes here, unnecessary to attempt any sort of general survey of Bahá'u'lláh's utilization of imagery in His revealed writings. His uses are as varied as the styles and purposes of His hundreds of tablets. But a few examples of this technique will illustrate the importance of understanding the metaphorical process when studying the writings of Bahá'u'lláh.

One of the most notable examples of an extended metaphor is the Seven Valleys, a richly allusive and highly imagistic discussion of the path to spirituality. Written in the form of a mystical treatise, the work itself uses as its organizing principle a journey through a variety of valleys as a metaphor for the stages in spiritual development. It is not a new device. Chaucer used a literal pilgrimage to symbolize the spiritual journey to the "New Jerusalem,"* and John Bunyan depicted salvation allegorically as a journey in *The Pilgrim's Progress*. Nevertheless, the journey is an effective framework. In Bahá'u'lláh's work there is a particular steed to carry the wayfarer through each valley—for the Valley of Search it is the steed of Patience, for the Valley of Love it is the steed of Pain, and

---

*At the end of the pilgrimage to Canterbury the Parson says:

And Jesus, by his grace, send me wit
To show you the way, on this journey,
To that same perfect glorious pilgrimage
Which is called the celestial city of Jerusalem.

My translation is based on the Fisher edition (348: X, 48–51).

so on. Each horse, of course, metaphorizes or symbolizes the primary attribute which the seeker must possess in order to traverse the valley successfully.

The succession of valleys to be traversed is only a device for the narrative framework. Within each valley Bahá'u'lláh uses allegorical anecdotes (such as the story of Majnún and Laylí) as well as traditions, poetry, Qur'anic verses, and a variety of other poetic devices to describe the essential nature and purpose of each stage in the spiritual ascent.

A number of prayers are also organized by one predominating image. For example, the morning prayers, while certainly appropriate to the literal morning time, also employ the repeated image of the morning time as a period of spiritual awakening during the Dispensation of a Manifestation. (For the same reason the early Bábí martyrs were designated "Dawn-Breakers.") Metaphorically, the morning prayers play off the notion of sleep as a state of spiritual deadness, in the same way that Bahá'u'lláh, in one of the Hidden Words, addresses the "Bond Slave of the World!" over whom "many a dawn hath the breeze of My loving-kindness wafted" and "found thee upon the bed of heedlessness fast asleep" (*Hidden Words* 33). Each "dawn" can represent the successive appearances of the Manifestations, signifying that those attached to the mundane world have been oblivious to the coming of more than one Prophet. The Sun, of course, represents the Manifestation. The light is the truth He brings, and the cycle of the day is the Dispensation itself.

Having established some of the possible meanings of "dawn" as a metaphor, we can discover a deeper level of meaning to a morning prayer by penetrating its literal surfaces. For example, let us see what happens in two paragraphs from the following prayer of Bahá'u'lláh:

> I give praise to Thee, O my God, that Thou has awakened me out of my sleep, and brought me forth after my disappearance, and raised me up from my slumber. I have wakened this morning with my face set toward the splendors of the Daystar of Thy Revelation, through Which the heavens of Thy power and Thy majesty have been illumined, acknowledging Thy signs, believing in Thy Book, and holding fast unto Thy Cord.

> I beseech Thee, by the potency of Thy will and the compelling power of Thy purpose, to make of what Thou didst reveal unto me in my sleep the surest foundation for the mansions of Thy love that are within the hearts of Thy loved ones, and the best instrument for the revelation of the tokens of Thy grace and Thy loving-kindness. (*Bahá'í Prayers* 118–19)

The prayer continues, but this passage is the heart of the metaphoric use of morning time. To take the prayer solely at its face or literal value seems to imply that we should try to recall something about a dream we have had, and indeed 'Abdu'l-Bahá does admonish us to pay attention to our dreams. But probing beneath these literal surfaces we find another level of meaning. If sleep is a state of our own heedlessness, we are praising God for having made us spiritually aware. But how can we assume that we are aware? Because we are praying the prayer. As we pray, we may literally be facing the point of the sun's rising as we turn to the Qiblih, but we are figuratively turning our attention to the "Daystar of Thy Revelation," Bahá'u'lláh Himself. Furthermore, the speaker, by acknowledging that he has "disappeared," implies that he had been awake before but had gone to sleep again, a possible allusion to the fact that most of us fail to maintain absolute constancy in following the light of truth.

What was it that was revealed to us in our sleep that "brought me forth after my disappearance"? Perhaps for each of us it is something different. For example, in the Long Obligatory Prayer of Bahá'u'lláh where we give thanks to God "that Thou hast aided me to remember Thee and to praise Thee. . . . " (*Bahá'í Prayers* 14), it is possibly the obligation to use the prayer that has awakened us from spiritual slumber and caused us to reaffirm our essential purpose in life and our just state of being. With the morning prayer it may be the same thing. But if we are praying, struggling with spiritual growth, something has aided us to arrive at that condition, and whatever it was has revived us and renewed our awareness of the metaphorical morning time in which we live.

Besides the prayers and meditations of Bahá'u'lláh, some of the most frequently noted extended metaphors occur in His Persian Hidden Words. The Persian language is, by tradition, a poetic language, and, as opposed to the Arabic language, a language less rich in synonym and, therefore, more apt to rely on imagery; hence it is not unexpected that the Persian section of the Hidden Words abounds in lush imagery. Some verses are simple and easily accessible: "In the garden of thy heart plant naught but the rose of love, and from the nightingale of affection and desire loosen not thy hold" (*Hidden Words* 23). Other verses are long, complex, and extremely difficult. But almost all illustrate well the importance of metaphor in understanding the many levels of meaning in the writings of Bahá'u'lláh.

One Hidden Word which is useful for our purposes employs an extended metaphor and three main vehicles—a sword, a sheath, and an artificer, or sword-maker:

> O My Servant! Thou art even as a finely tempered sword concealed in the darkness of its sheath and its value hidden from the artificer's knowledge. Wherefore come forth from the sheath of self and desire that thy worth may be made resplendent and manifest unto all the world. (*Hidden Words* 47)

Here Bahá'u'lláh has given us a start by filling in one of the three missing tenors in this equation—the sheath is "self and desire." Moreover, since the passage is addressed to a "servant," we can assume, perhaps, that the sword is a Bahá'í. We can also assume that the artificer is God or the Manifestation (God as Creator or the Manifestation Who has, in effect, recreated us). But the equation is still not really solved because we do not know why the sword, the sheath, and the artificer are compared, what the metaphor is meant to demonstrate, until we consider more carefully the tone and nature of the comparison.

The servant is being criticized for remaining in the "sheath of self and desire"—that much we can understand—but why a sword, and a finely tempered one at that? A sword, especially when finely tempered, is a practical instrument, a weapon of war. The servants of God are also meant to be practically useful—no longer monks in monasteries, but active in the world, warring against iniquity and injustice. To make themselves known to God, they must act, must use the perfections which lie dormant. Here we may be reminded of the many passages which extol the lofty possibilities of the human spirit. When this potential is manifest in physical action, the spiritual capacity latent within all men becomes "manifest unto all the world." This is a particularly plausible interpretation since this passage is near the end of the volume, where we find similar exhortations for the "servant" to act: "Ye are the trees of My garden; ye must give forth goodly and wondrous fruits, that ye yourselves and others may profit therefrom" (*Hidden Words* 50–51). The penultimate Hidden Word, also addressed to "My Servant," states the converse: "The basest of men are they that yield no fruit on earth. Such men are verily counted as among the dead, nay better are the dead in the sight of God than those idle and worthless souls" (*Hidden Words* 51).

Of course, the examples from the Seven Valleys, the morning prayer, and the Hidden Words are but a very few of the infinite variety of uses of metaphorical language in the writings of Bahá'u'lláh, each with its own possibilities for meaning. We need not be students of literature or poetry to understand or appreciate the writings of Bahá'u'lláh, but we must have something of a poetic soul to grasp the inner essence of what the Prophet means, if by "poetic" we mean the capacity to "see with thine own eyes and not through the eyes of others. . . . " (*Hidden Words* 4).

But it is not only in the more poetic tablets that Bahá'u'lláh uses imagery. Even in the Kitáb-i-Íqán, which is a relatively straightforward essay, or in the Kitáb-i-Aqdas, the repository of Bahá'u'lláh's laws, there appears image upon image. Sometimes it is only a word or phrase, but often the figures are several lines in length. We need glimpse only a few of the numerous examples from the prefatory passages of the Kitáb-i-Aqdas to see this:

> Know assuredly that My commandments are the lamps of My loving providence among My servants, and the keys of My mercy for My creatures. . . .
> Think not that We have revealed unto you a mere code of laws. Nay, rather, We have unsealed the choice Wine with the fingers of might and power. (Bahá'u'lláh, *Synopsis* 11–12)

> Whenever My laws appear like the sun in the heaven of Mine

utterance, they must be faithfully obeyed by all, though My decree be such as to cause the heaven of every religion to be cleft asunder. (*Synopsis* 12)

In these excerpts Bahá'u'lláh compares His laws to lamps, keys, choice wine, and the sun—and these are but a meager sampling of the quantity, quality, and complexity of the imagery in Bahá'u'-lláh's less metaphorical revealed works.

But in addition to using metaphor in the language of their teachings, the Manifestations utilize metaphor in prophecy. Many Christians are still trying to discover the key to the symbols and figurative imagery in Christ's allusions to His return, and speculation abounds regarding the intricate symbolism of the Book of Revelation. Likewise, Muslim scholars have devoted themselves to interpreting the veiled traditions regarding the Promised Qá'im and the Mihdí, just as the Jews have awaited the fulfillment of Messianic prophecy.

Perhaps because prophecy is such an important link from one revelation to the next, Bahá'u'lláh devotes a substantial portion of the Kitáb-i-Íqán to a study of the nature of prophecy. In fact, because it is replete with examples of the use of recurring metaphors and symbols and because it discusses the rationale underlying the use of prophecy, the Kitáb-i-Íqán could be considered a casebook study on the subject. More specifically, Bahá'u'lláh discusses the use of metaphorical language as He explains vehicles such as *suns, heaven, clouds, smoke,* and *angels.* He also discusses some of the reasons for the intentional obfuscation which this metaphoric and symbolic language creates. For example, He states that the purpose of a Manifestation's refusing to describe the time, the place, and the personality of a succeeding Manifestation has been to test the hearts of seekers. If people were allowed to discover the Manifestation by a name or physical aspect only, they would not be required to ascertain the spiritual nature of what they seek. Some might turn to the Manifestation to achieve fame or use His power for their benefit. Those who possess temporal power and authority might view the Manifestation as a threat to their positions and might attempt to destroy Him, as did Herod with Christ, Hájí Mírzá Áqásí with the Báb, and Náṣiri'd-Dín Sháh with Bahá'u'lláh.

But because the identity of the Manifestation is concealed in prophecy, we must be spiritually aware in order to discover Him. If we understand power and authority only in literal or physical terms, we will probably look for a physically impressive figure or someone who has achieved temporal power. In short, we may be totally oblivious to the Manifestation.

In the laws of the Manifestation we can find still another use of metaphor, besides the imagery in the laws we have already noted, and that is the metaphorical value or inner significance of the actions these laws require. The laws have the pragmatic benefits of requiring sane and healthy responses to existential dilemmas, but they also force us to act out dramatically in the physical world what we are trying to accomplish in the spiritual world.

The correlation between healthy actions and spiritual growth may not be so apparent with the laws which are basically restrictive and prohibitive in nature, but it is there all the same. For example, the Jews may have thought the Mosaic dietary laws arbitrary, but they followed them anyway. In doing so, they practiced reverence for the authority of Moses and His beneficent intentions. Now that science has discovered how various diseases are contracted, we can understand the scientific basis for Moses' laws and realize how these so-called restrictions were actually a source of liberation. Therefore, in perceiving the divine logic in the laws governing physical action and learning to follow the conduct prescribed by the Manifestations, we are training ourselves to have faith in the ultimate liberation which the ostensible restriction imposes. It is then possible for us to apply this lesson to our compliance with spiritual laws—we begin to accept the laws of the Manifestation as benign guidance and a loving gift. Like their counterparts in the phenomenal world—the physical laws—God's divine ordinances are thus pragmatic and logical and liberating. Furthermore, as we act them out, we are enabled to appreciate dramatically or metaphorically the beneficence of God in educating us:

> Say: True liberty consisteth in man's submission unto My commandments, little as ye know it. Were men to observe that which We have sent down unto them from the Heaven of Revelation, they would, of a certainty, attain unto perfect liberty. Happy is the man

that hath apprehended the Purpose of God in whatever He hath revealed from the Heaven of His Will, that pervadeth all created things. (Bahá'u'lláh, *Synopsis* 25)

Understood in the light of Bahá'u'lláh's statement on liberty, the laws of the Manifestation never prevent the full and complete utilization of the physical experience. On the contrary, even those laws which imply restriction ultimately encourage the most fulfilling use of it. Stated another way, the laws of the Manifestation enable one to experience the metaphorical value of the physical world, even when the follower is unaware that he is doing anything other than obeying divine authority.

The laws which provide creative use of our physical lives reinforce the metaphorical value of that experience perhaps even more obviously than the laws of admonition and prohibition. Because the laws governing our physical lives change from one Manifestation to the next so that they accurately describe the relative progress of man, this progress itself is essentially metaphorical in nature in that a society acts out literally a figurative or spiritual condition. When the law creates institutions, organizational structures, and codes of behavior which foster advancement, the law itself becomes an integral part of our efforts to dramatize spiritual progress.

In addition to the long-range benefit of laws governing our physical lives, such laws have the immediate effect of creating for the individual an atmosphere or environment conducive to spiritual growth. We are only beginning to understand the profound influence which our physical environment has on our mental, emotional, and spiritual conditions, but the Manifestations have always understood this relationship and have reflected that understanding in their laws, whether the law describes how we conduct human relationships, organize our lives, or care for our bodies:

> External cleanliness, although it is but a physical thing, hath a great influence upon spirituality. For example, although sound is but the vibrations of the air which affect the tympanum of the ear, and vibrations of the air are but an accident among the accidents which depend upon the air, consider how much marvelous notes or a

charming song influence the spirits! ('Abdu'l-Bahá, *Tablets of Abdul-Baha Abbas* 3:581–82)

As the laws gradually enhance our ability to manifest spiritual concepts in daily action, they participate in the largest and most important metaphorical exercise on this planet, the gradual but unrelenting establishment of a spiritual kingdom translated into physical form. Seen in this light, the entire Bahá'í administrative order, its institutions, and procedures, are dramatic expressions of this process.

Finally, many of the laws themselves are metaphorical exercises. When Christ wished to teach the abstract concept of love to His followers, He ordained a law to dramatize that quality:

> "You have heard that it was said, 'An eye for an eye and a tooth for a tooth.' But I say to you, Do not resist one who is evil. But if any one strikes you on the right cheek, turn to him the other also; and if any one would sue you and take your coat, let him have your cloak as well; and if any one forces you to go one mile, go with him two miles. Give to him who begs from you, and do not refuse him who would borrow from you.
>
> ". . . For if you love those who love you, what reward have you? Do not even the tax collectors do the same?" (Matt. 38–42, 46)

Likewise, while Bahá'u'lláh teaches us the abstract concepts of the unity of mankind and the equality of men and women, He also provides humankind, through His creative laws, with the dramatic institutions which enable it to act out the spiritual law with physical action. Properly understood and perceived, many of the laws of the Manifestations are similarly dramaturgical in nature, metaphorical devices by which we express with action what we wish to feel and understand on a spiritual level. Sometimes the understanding precedes the dramatization; sometimes the reverse is true. The point is that in studying the nature of the Manifestation Himself, His actions, His use of language, or His laws, we can observe the metaphorical tie between spiritual growth and physical performance as each reinforces the other in a pattern of continuous growth.

The Metaphorical Lessons in Negative Experience

Obviously it would be erroneous to imply that all spiritual growth results from the willful application of the metaphorical process. A substantial portion of our experience is beyond our control. In addition, much of our most memorable experience in this life centers around negative events, whether they be injustices suffered at the hands of others or simply the myriad unfortunate accidents that are the lot of mortal beings. But though such experiences may not be the result of our intentional application of the metaphorical process, we can still extract from them some of our most significant metaphorical lessons.

To begin with, negative experience can be generally classified in two broad categories. First, there are accidents like those suffered by Job, events we might describe in terms of chance (such as natural disasters). Second, there are negative experiences resulting from the iniquity, maliciousness, or injustice of others, the sort of experience that provoked Boethius to write his treatise.

The traditional problem in understanding experience of the first category is an obvious one. If God loves us and has the power to prevent such events, why does He not do so? Or, following what we have just observed about the benign intent of physical reality, what is the metaphorical value of such experience? If accidents are part of the punishment inherent in the system of rewards and punishments, how do we account for the death of the innocent? Furthermore, if God in His foreknowledge is aware that a chance disaster is going to occur, it will occur; therefore, the event seems predestined since it cannot be averted. In the face of such reasoning and the unfortunate events that often befall humankind, many have found belief in a loving Deity quite difficult. Others, such as Harold Kushner in his study of theodicy *When Bad Things Happen to Good People,* conclude that God "is limited in what He can do by laws of nature and by the evolution of human nature and human moral freedom" (134). Juxtaposed to wars and other unspeakable sorts of inhumanity, our view of physical reality as a just and exquisite teaching device may seem to falter and fail.

To respond even briefly to these concerns we need first to clarify what we mean by *evil,* because we tend to classify experience too broadly. We categorize as evil all things which seem negative, from man's immorality to thunder and flood, from disease to political tyranny, from insects to sharks. Such a tendency is understandable, for we logically assume that if these things are in God's universe, He is somehow responsible for them.

As we noted in chapter 2, from a Bahá'í point of view there is only one sort of occurrence which can legitimately be called "evil"—man's willful rejection of his divine purpose. Bahá'u'lláh states that "the source of all evil is for man to turn away from his Lord and set his heart on things ungodly" (*Tablets of Bahá'u'lláh* 156). This is very specific. Yet "evil" in this sense does not include the failure to recognize the Manifestation because of improper education or other forces beyond one's control:

> But in a place where the commands of a Prophet are not known, and where the people do not act in conformity with the divine instructions, . . . from the point of view of religion they are excused because the divine command has not been delivered to them. ('Abdu'l-Bahá, *Some Answered Questions* 267)

Stated another way, there is no evil inherent in God's creation except for those events which proceed from man's willful rejection of goodness. Thus when 'Abdu'l-Bahá states that "in creation there is no evil; all is good" ('Abdu'l-Bahá, *Some Answered Questions* 215), He means that there is no source of evil. Terms like *sin, Satan, evil,* and *wickedness* appear in the Bahá'í writings, just as they have appeared in the scriptures of previous revelations, but they designate an action, not an essence. The term *Satan,* for example, is usually a metaphor for the temptation to be self-consumed, selfish, to glory in one's own personality: "God has never created an evil spirit; all such ideas and nomenclature are symbols expressing the mere human or earthly nature of man" ('Abdu'l-Bahá, *Promulgation* 295).

Evil is thus the absence of goodness in the same way that darkness is the absence of light. Nevertheless, there are significant results caused by the absence of light or heat or goodness. The turning away from the source of all life can cause changes in condition which are sometimes momentous and frightening. They need to be understood and described; and, consequently, we use powerful, vivid metaphors to portray these effects. By analogy, in the physical world cold is but the absence of heat, not the presence of a cold energy, not the influence of a source of coldness. Yet one obviously needs effective phrases to describe the absence of heat because it can exert untoward influence on us. If we were to go to the Arctic wastes, the very lack of heat might become so palpable that we would find it absurd to say that an essentially nonexistent force was destroying our very lives.

The point is that we need words, images, metaphors to portray laws in motion. In one sense Hitler and the destruction he wrought resulted from a rejection of the laws of God which are the source of energy, and yet we need to portray adequately the wretched and heart-rending results of that turning away from truth. Consequently, we resort to metaphorical expressions which describe this appearance in history of an apparent source of iniquity and injustice.

Similarly, the Manifestations of the past, wishing to convey spiritual states of being, have turned to metaphors for evil, not because the Manifestations wished to distort the reality of a spiritual existence but because such devices were the best means by which man could understand the abstractions. They frequently described pride in terms of an iniquitous tempter, a Satan; spiritual growth in the next world in terms of an idyllic pastoral abode, a paradise; and spiritual degradation in terms of physical torment, a hell:

> Even the materialists have testified in their writings to the wisdom of these divinely-appointed Messengers, and have regarded the references made by the Prophets to Paradise, to hell fire, to future reward and punishment, to have been actuated by a desire to educate and uplift the souls of men. (Bahá'u'lláh, *Gleanings* 158)

In one sense, then, evil is the result of man's willful acts; Bahá'u'lláh writes that "were men to abide by and observe the divine teachings, every trace of evil would be banished from the face of the earth" (*Tablets of Bahá'u'lláh* 176).

And yet not all events we term "evil" can be defined as the logical consequence of our turning away from goodness. How do we account for the suffering of the innocent and for tests that befall us which seem to have no relationship to anything we have done? While not "evil" according to our precise definition, these events are still negative, unfortunate, ostensibly unjust.

There are several major principles in the Bahá'í writings which urge us toward a solution to these substantial dilemmas. For example, God is not restricted to this life in the working out of justice in our individual lives, nor to a certain span of time for working out justice in history, as we have noted earlier. This observation is obvious but crucial because it means that we cannot possibly evaluate what befalls us or anyone else in terms of whether it ultimately results in justice or injustice or whether it is harmful or beneficial. As we have discussed, since our fruition is destined for another plane of existence, we can hardly judge what does and does not benefit that process any more than a fruit tree could evaluate the end result of its own pruning.

From our limited point of view the death of the infant is pointless and unjust, as is the suffering of the innocent. Yet it is clear in the Bahá'í writings that these infants are cared for, as are all who suffer innocently:

> These infants are under the shadow of the favor of God; and as they have not committed any sin and are not soiled with the impurities of the world of nature, they are the centers of the manifestation of bounty, and the Eye of Compassion will be turned upon them. ('Abdu'l-Bahá, *Some Answered Questions* 240)

> As to the subject of babes and infants and weak ones who are afflicted by the hands of oppressors: This contains great wisdom and this subject is of paramount importance. In brief, for those souls there is a recompense in another world and many details are connected with this matter. For those souls that suffering is the greatest mercy of God. Verily that mercy of the Lord is far better and preferable to all the comfort of this world and the growth and development of this place of mortality. ('Abdu'l-Bahá, *Tablets of Abdul-Baha Abbas* 2:337–38)

Properly comprehended, true suffering in relation to such events is on the part of those who remain behind, deprived of the companionship of souls who have departed or who have become consumed by illness. In reality, we grieve for ourselves, because from the passage above it is clear that those who die prematurely are in no way impaired by the experience. Likewise we are assured that those who, because of mental or physical illness, no longer seem to us to be progressing spiritually are not ultimately affected negatively by such experience:

> man is exalted above, and is independent of all infirmities of body or mind. That a sick person showeth signs of weakness is due to the hindrances that interpose themselves between his soul and his body, for the soul itself remaineth unaffected by any bodily ailments. (Bahá'u'lláh, *Gleanings* 153–54)

To fail to grasp the essential realization of the Bahá'í paradigm that life is a continuum and not limited to the physical world is to see as ludicrous most martyrdoms and all the indignities which the Manifestations willingly endure:

> How could such Souls have consented to surrender themselves unto their enemies if they believed all the worlds of God to have been reduced to this earthly life? Would they have willingly suffered such afflictions and torments as no man hath ever experienced or witnessed? (Bahá'u'lláh, *Gleanings* 158)

But we are still left with a dilemma regarding God's intervention. If God foreknows our suffering, is He not somehow responsible? Why does He not intervene to prevent our suffering so that we can reap the benefits of the metaphorical classroom He has so wonderfully devised?

To a certain extent this subject transcends the purpose of this discussion, but several important responses resolve some of this matter. We have already noted that God's foreknowledge of a thing is not the cause of its occurrence, any more than our knowledge of the operation of a physical law causes that law to be enforced. But once foreknowing our suffering, why does God not prevent it?

One response is that God does intervene, repeatedly, consistently, progressively, even personally. In the larger context God precisely directs the course of history, sending successive Manifestations according to the ancient Covenant between God and man, not because man is deserving of such bestowals, but because God is forgiving. We are also assured that the same assistance is available in our personal lives if we but ask for it: "God is merciful. In His mercy He answers the prayers of all His servants when according to His supreme wisdom it is necessary" ('Abdu'l-Bahá, *Promulgation* 247). And since it is God's intent to educate and help us, we can assume that He deems it "necessary" whenever it is beneficial for us. We may not always be able to predict when or how God will intervene in our lives or in what way He will respond to our entreaties; we only know that intervention will eventually occur if we earnestly seek it.

A second response to the question of why God does not prevent our negative experience is that more often than not the events we perceive to be adverse have immense capacity to educate us. Such tests are part and parcel of the whole metaphorical scheme by which we are spiritually transformed by our physical experience. To understand the merits or rewards of such negative experiences, we can return to our earlier analogy of the athlete. To the athlete, stress, even stress to the point of pain, is not perceived as negative because he is aware of his goal and how the seemingly negative experience of training will enable him to attain his goal—he perceives the end in the beginning. For our own education in the metaphorical classroom of physical reality testing is similarly crucial; indeed, the Bahá'í writings are replete with discussions affirming this fact:

Tests are benefits from God, for which we should thank Him. Grief and sorrow do not come to us by chance, they are sent to us by the Divine Mercy for our own perfecting. ('Abdu'l-Bahá, *Paris Talks* 50)

The mind and spirit of man advance when he is tried by suffering. The more the ground is ploughed the better the seed will grow, the better the harvest will be. ('Abdu'l-Bahá, *Paris Talks* 178)

As to tests, these are inevitable. Hast thou not heard and read how there appeared trials from God in the days of Jesus, and thereafter, and how the winds of tests became severe? Even the glorious Peter was not relieved from the claws of trials. He wavered, then he repented and mourned the mourning of a bereaved one. . . . ('Abdu'l-Bahá, qtd. in Bahá'u'lláh and 'Abdu'l-Bahá, *Divine Art of Living* 86–87)

The teachings of Bahá'u'lláh thus respond to the questions raised by both sorts of negative experience and thereby resolve the dilemmas presented in the Book of Job and in *The Consolation of Philosophy*. As an integral part of the metaphorical acting out of virtue, testing assays the degree to which we have truly understood and habituated spiritual attributes: "Were it not for tests, pure gold could not be distinguished from the impure" ('Abdu'l-Bahá, qtd. in Bahá'u'lláh and 'Abdu'l-Bahá, *Divine Art of Living* 87). No doubt it is for this reason that "the tests and trials of God take place in this world, not in the world of the Kingdom" ('Abdu'l-Bahá, *Selections* 194). And yet, even though we are assured that through suffering we "will attain to an eternal happiness" ('Abdu'l-Bahá, *Paris Talks* 178), and that "soon (God) thy Lord will bestow upon thee that which shall satisfy thee" ('Abdu'l-Bahá, *Tablets of Abdul-Baha Abbas* 1:98), we are also told that our refusal to recognize our weaknesses ensures that we will be subjected to the same test occurring with greater severity:

> Tests are a means by which a soul is measured as to its fitness, and proven out by its own acts. God knows its fitness beforehand, and also its unpreparedness, but man, with an ego, would not believe himself unfit unless proof were given him. Consequently his susceptibility to evil is proven to him when he falls into the tests, and the tests are continued until the soul realizes its own unfitness, then remorse and regret tend to root out the weakness.
>
> The same test comes again in greater degree, until it is shown that a former weakness has become a strength, and the power to overcome evil has been established. ('Abdu'l-Bahá, "Worst Enemies" 45)

Assuming, then, that we can accept even the negative experiences as part of the divine plan for educating us, we are still left with a final question which encompasses the whole process—why is a physical existence necessary in the first place? For even if the process of spiritual development and enlightenment works as planned, why could there not be a simpler, easier, less painful method of accomplishing the same task? In short, if God is omnipotent and can create us in whatever way He wishes, why did He not create us already spiritualized, already in a state of understanding?

If the question seems presumptuous, it is not. Bahá'u'lláh deals with this very issue when He explains that God could have made things simpler, but His purpose is to force us to search independently, to choose for ourselves the path that is the source of our advancement:

> He Who is the Day Spring of Truth is, no doubt, fully capable of rescuing from such remoteness wayward souls and of causing them to draw nigh unto His court and attain His Presence. "If God had pleased He had surely made all men one people." His purpose, however, is to enable the pure in spirit and the detached in heart to ascend, by virtue of their own innate powers, unto the shores of the Most Great Ocean, that thereby they who seek the Beauty of the All-Glorious may be distinguished and separated from the wayward and perverse. (*Gleanings* 71)

To create already spiritualized beings would be to produce automatons incapable of progressing on their own or of appreciating what they have because they would not have discovered it for themselves or experienced anything else. Furthermore, were the spiritual reality more apparent on this plane of existence, man would have no sense of personal recognition and perception, since the meaning of reality would be obvious to all alike.

By veiling spiritual reality in a metaphorical physical garb, by removing the essential reality of things one step from the vision of men, God has enabled us to have every opportunity to attain spiritual knowledge and to have the bounty of recognition, and an awareness of the contrast between illusion and reality. The change from darkness to light, from ignorance to understanding, can provide more than a few moments of elation and reward; it can provide the impetus for continuing progress and the tools of discernment with which to carry out that objective.

But as we will see more completely in the next chapter, the most important justification for our having to learn initially about spiritual reality through physical metaphors is that we must each learn from our physical environment how to keep progressing during our existence beyond this world. Were there only two levels of existence in the next world, a heaven for those who succeed and a hell for those who fail, or even if there were various sorts of strata within these categories, possibly God could have created man sufficiently spiritualized for a heavenly existence, and we would not have lost much. But the Bahá'í writings reveal that there is no static existence in this world or the next, no relegation of the soul to an eternal abode within some fixed category of existence. Whether in this world or the next, we are constantly changing, and the point of transition we call *death* does not terminate the process of our spiritual development, nor does it end man's need to utilize the spiritual faculties he has developed in this life.

The distinction between the Bahá'í view of the afterlife and some traditional conceptions of other religions is, as we will see, a crucial one. Were it our destiny to attain one unchanging state of being, one explicit level of growth, such development could conceivably be accomplished without the metaphorical classroom, or else with an exacting canon of rules and guidelines to program us for growth. But because it is our nature as human souls, whether in this life or in the next, to be constantly changing, what was an adequate guideline yesterday may be insufficient for us tomorrow. In addition, since no two people are in exactly the same condition, each individual's plan of spiritual development must be distinctly tailored to the conditions of his or her soul—what we are trying to develop are faculties of discernment and judgment so that each of us has a degree of spiritual autonomy, the desire to foster our own spiritual advancement, and the tools to carry out that progress. We must be capable of choosing on a daily basis that point of moderation between the extremes—the courage that lies between foolhardiness and cowardice, the joy between oppressive serious- ness and insipid frivolity, the wise guidance between unfeeling judiciality and permissiveness.

The objective of our education, then, is not a blind adherence to dogma. Bahá'u'lláh admonishes us to evaluate our progress on a daily basis and, with each new assessment, decide what is progressive for us and yet not so far beyond our grasp that we will frustrate our own determination to strive. Certainly considering what lessons we can extract from our ostensibly negative and painful experiences is an integral and vital part of this daily evaluation. No handbook on personal conduct could do this for us, could take into account the exigencies of our individual lives. Perhaps it is for this reason that Bahá'u'lláh revealed relatively few laws regarding personal behavior but created instead decision-making institutions with the capacity to consider all the variables in a given situation and to make appropriate decisions about a course of action based on those considerations.

Detachment

It becomes clear, then, that our spiritual development is largely contingent on the development of spiritual faculties by means of metaphorical exercises provided for our advancement. It is equally clear that to learn how to use our metaphorical classroom, we must rely on our own volition and, at least in the initial stages of our growth, participate actively, enthusiastically, but wisely in the phenomenal world. But as we participate, we must be wary of one final requisite for the proper and healthy use of our ingenious instructional device—detachment.

As a quality, the term *detachment* denotes the capacity to use physical metaphors without becoming overly attracted to, infatuated with, or involved in the literal teaching device. As a process, the term implies a gradual relinquishing of our reliance on the physical vehicle to accomplish spiritual development. Our use of physical metaphors is purposely short-lived. Like water which primes a pump, physical lessons serve to initiate the process of spiritual development. But as our growth progresses, we have less and less need to relate directly to the physical metaphor in order to understand the abstraction and to set ourselves in motion.

In the beginning we feel inseparable from the literal vehicle through which our souls find expression. Our self-image and self-respect are often inextricably bound up in our physical presence and appearance: Are we tall, short, fat, or thin? Are we beautiful and strong? Are we acceptable to others? But as we mature, we should learn to relinquish our dependency on our physical selves in order to evaluate our lives. In time we come to evaluate ourselves in terms of the spiritual qualities we have attempted to express through the vehicle of the body. And in time we come to depend less and less on relating to spiritual reality through the phenomenal metaphor.

We are told in the holy writings of all religions that one of the most dangerous impediments to spiritual advancement is the love of self. Metaphorically, this love is expressed through attachment to the vehicle for the self, the physical body. When we become obsessed with our physical appearance, we may be forgetting that our essential reality is our soul, which temporarily expresses itself through the body. If we love the vehicle for itself or see the vehicle as synonymous with the tenor, we disregard the intended metaphorical purpose of physical reality.

To safeguard against just such a misuse, the Creator has provided us with a number of metaphorical reminders of our true nature. The most intriguing of these is the aging process. At almost the precise point our physical body has reached its peak of perfection, we are as intellectual and spiritual beings only beginning to develop. As we begin to strive for spiritual growth, our metaphorical self begins to crumble before our eyes. If we have missed the point of our earthly assignment and have become too attached to this metaphorical vehicle, the divinely ordained aging process will eventually teach us that our attachment is doomed. In due time we will become detached from our metaphorical self whether we like it or not.

But if we follow our lessons well in this "Great Workshop," the deterioration of our physical selves together with the decrease in our ability to utilize the physical classroom will parallel a corresponding increase in our spiritual faculties so that at the moment of transition from the terrestrial world to the "real world," our final detachment from the worn-out metaphor will occur at the precise instant that we can no longer use it anyway:

> The purpose underlying their revelation hath been to educate all men, that they may, at the hour of death, ascend, in the utmost purity and

sanctity and with absolute detachment, to the throne of the Most High. (Bahá'u'lláh, *Gleanings* 157)

And what will be the nature of our experience in the life after death? How will our efforts here affect our experience there? This is naturally the most intriguing question of all. For if our purpose here is to transform ourselves in preparation for our birth into spiritual existence, we must presume that what we do in the physical world has a direct and dramatic bearing on our success in the afterlife.

The Eternal Consequences of the Physical Experience **4**

Didst thou behold immortal sovereignty, thou wouldst strive to pass from this fleeting world. But to conceal the one from thee and to reveal the other is a mystery which none but the pure in heart can comprehend.

—Bahá'u'lláh

If one point has become clear thus far in our examination of the nature and purpose of physical reality, it is the forceful emphasis in the Bahá'í writings on the strategic relationship in our physical lives between our actions and our spiritual development. The Bahá'í teachings are very existential in this regard. In no sense is the physical life viewed merely as a period of waiting until one enters a spiritual realm. The physical world, properly understood, is an integral part of spiritual reality, indeed, a precise expression of that world. But if our spiritual progress in physical life is greatly affected by our actions, we might reasonably assume that our overall performance on earth would have a significant effect on our existence in the afterlife. The nature of that relationship between our earthly lives and our eternal spiritual destiny is our final concern in examining the spiritual purpose of physical reality.

As we have noted, in the Bahá'í paradigm of divine justice the departure from the physical world is not really a separate venture, not an afterlife, but a continuation of the same life. While noble aspirations and actions in the physical world are extremely important in determining the spiritual condition of one entering the next stage of existence, life after death is not merely the eternal result of efforts made in the physical phase of existence. For if the physical life has its paradigm for spiritual growth, so does the life to come.

A belief in a continuation of growth after death is not necessarily comforting inasmuch as it implies that the arduous efforts at spiritual transformation in our physical life lead only to further challenges in the next stage of our existence. Furthermore, such a reality implies that there is ultimately no escape from ourselves—if we are dissatisfied with what we are now, we will most likely be just as disappointed after death. But certainly the nature of those challenges is significantly changed since the trials which often account for the greater part of our struggle in this life—physical pain, financial hardship, and the like—will have vanished.

We can only guess at how our lives proceed in the next world insofar as a regimen of spiritual development is concerned, but in the Bahá'í teachings we can discover some profound and important realities about that existence and, more to the point, about the relationship between this life and the next, between what we do in the physical part of our existence and what we experience in our lives beyond this world.

The Fear of Death

Repeatedly in His writings Bahá'u'lláh emphasizes that were we to understand adequately the operation of God's creation, we would discard our fears of death: "I have made death a messenger of joy to thee. Wherefore dost thou grieve?" (*Hidden Words* 11). Nevertheless, most people continue to fear death for many reasons. If we do not believe in a life after death, we may dread the prospect of nonexistence. If we believe in a continuation of our lives, we may be concerned about what sort of judgment awaits us. If we are dissatisfied with who we are or what we have become, we may fear the inability to escape from our own consciousness.

But if there is nothing to fear—if, as Bahá'u'lláh says, death is "a messenger of joy"—we cannot help asking why so little is revealed to us about that existence. Why, in other words, are we not given ample detail about how our development will continue?

One hindrance, of course, is the difficulty in portraying a dimension with which we have so little direct experience in this life. In the same way, we ourselves might find it impossible to describe to a child in the womb of its mother the reality of this world. From our examination of the metaphorical nature of physical reality we can also conclude that concealment of the afterlife serves to test us, to stretch us, as a wise teacher might withhold the answer to a problem in order to motivate the student to acquire the tools for further learning.

Bahá'u'lláh states explicitly that one purpose in concealing that reality is to protect us. Were we adequately informed about the life to come, we would not be able to restrain ourselves from attaining it and would abandon the proper uses of this stage of our development:

> If any man be told that which hath been ordained for such a soul [one which is "sanctified from the vain imaginings of the peoples of the world"] in the worlds of God, . . . his whole being will instantly blaze out in his great longing to attain that most exalted, that sanctified and resplendent station. . . . (*Gleanings* 156)

But Bahá'ís do not live isolated from the rest of the world. In spite of such forceful reassurances about the next stage of existence, it is easy to fall prey to the prevailing attitudes regarding death. In the foreword to Elisabeth Kübler-Ross' work *Death: The Final Stage of Growth,* Joseph and Laurie Braga observe how "death is a subject that is evaded, ignored, and denied by our youth-worshipping, progress-oriented society. It is almost as if we have taken on death as just another disease to be conquered" (x).

When several years ago a number of books began to be published that attempted to document the afterlife experiences of patients who had experienced "clinical" death, we might have thought that attitudes about death would have been dramatically affected. Such studies seemed to vindicate belief in the continuation of the soul and for the most part portray the afterlife as a positive experience. For example, Elisabeth Kübler-Ross, perhaps the most widely acclaimed writer and authority in the emerging field of death counseling, stated in one interview that there is no need to fear death since God does not judge us—our earthly performance has no bearing on how we are received:

Discussing the aspects of an afterlife as described by patients, Mrs. Kübler-Ross remarked that those involved in the research were puzzled that there seemed to be no fear or punishment connected with death.

"It seemed that a Hitler and a Mother Theresa got the same treatment. Then, we realized that God is not judgmental. We are the ones who discriminate." ("Dr. Kübler-Ross")

Views such as those of Kübler-Ross might make us wonder if we are not being provided with the knowledge to which Bahá'u'lláh alludes when He states:

In the treasuries of the knowledge of God there lieth concealed a knowledge which, when applied, will largely, though not wholly, eliminate fear. This knowledge, however, should be taught from childhood, as it will greatly aid in its elimination. Whatever decreaseth fear increaseth courage. (*Epistle* 32)

When Shoghi Effendi was asked about this passage, his secretary replied on his behalf, "Unfortunately it would seem that the knowledge 'which could largely eliminate fear' has not been disclosed or identified by Bahá'u'lláh, so we do not know what it is" ("Excerpts from Letters" 3). Therefore, we cannot ascertain with any certainty what was intended, but the remarkable attitude of the Bahá'í martyrs in the past and the present might seem to corroborate this knowledge as dealing with life after death. Perhaps the martyrs were eager to sacrifice their lives because, as a result of their determination not to recant their faith even in the face of death, they had a vision of the afterlife so palpable and intimate that they had absolutely no fear of the joyous reality that lay before them only minutes or hours away.* Their actions still required immense courage and staunch faith, but perhaps such a divine bestowal helped them conquer the utter terror of humiliation, torture, and often the mutilation of themselves and their own families.

---

*This observation comes to me secondhand but is purported to have been suggested by the Hand of the Cause of God A. Q. Faizí.

The martyrs' fearlessness regarding death is reflected in and somewhat corroborated by the collected accounts of people who had experienced clinical death. In the best known of these compilations, Raymond A. Moody's *Life After Life*, subjects describe an inner peace and a fearlessness about life as a consequence of what they perceive to be their personal experience in the afterlife. In addition, these subjects no longer seem worried about the prospect of death itself.

Kübler-Ross indicates as a result of her observations from dealing with terminally ill and dying patients that an accurate understanding of death would reveal nothing to fear in the transition to another stage in our continuing existence:

> Death is the final stage of growth in this life. There is no total death. Only the body dies. The self or spirit, or whatever you may wish to label it, is eternal. . . .
> Death, in this context, may be viewed as the curtain between the existence that we are conscious of and one that is hidden from us until we raise that curtain. (*Death* 166)

But even if we are assured that further existence awaits us, our fears are not assuaged unless we are *also* confident that such an existence will be a positive one. As Hamlet notes, it is

> the dread of something after death,
> The undiscover'd country from whose bourn
> No traveller returns, puzzles the will
> And makes us rather bear those ills we have
> Than fly to others that we know not of? (III.i.78–82)

Our primary concern, then, is the nature of that afterlife experience as it relates to our physical lives—the correlation between our physical performance (our metaphorical acting out of spiritual attributes) and our eternal well-being. If there is a causal relationship, naturally our feelings about the physical plane of existence would be profoundly affected by this knowledge, just as would be our anticipation of our future existence.

The Passage to the Next World

While Bahá'u'lláh withholds from us any complete portrayal of the afterlife experience, the Bahá'í writings contain a logically consistent portrait or paradigm of the passage to the next life. By comparing that paradigm with more of Raymond A. Moody's findings, we can begin to understand something about what the initial stages of the afterlife may be like and what the purpose of physical reality is in relation to that afterlife experience.

Although Moody's study *Life After Life* is an unpretentious and somewhat unscientific collection of evidence, his model of the afterlife experience offers a useful delineation of the process of transition from the physical world to the next world, a model that has since been confirmed by other studies. At the outset Moody presents a composite description of the afterlife experience, a synthesis of the most frequently recurring ingredients, since not all the experiences follow exactly the same pattern:

> A man is dying and, as he reaches the point of greatest physical distress, he hears himself pronounced dead by his doctor. He begins to hear an uncomfortable noise, a loud ringing or buzzing, and at the same time feels himself moving very rapidly through a long dark tunnel. After this, he suddenly finds himself outside of his own physical body, but still in the immediate physical environment, and he sees his own body from a distance, as though he is a spectator. He watches the resuscitation attempt from this unusual vantage point and is in a state of emotional upheaval.
>
> After a while, he collects himself and becomes more accustomed to his odd condition. He notices that he still has a "body," but one of a very different nature and with very different powers from the physical body he has left behind. Soon other things begin to happen. Others come to meet and to help him. He glimpses the spirits of relatives and friends who have already died, and a loving, warm spirit of a kind he has never encountered before—a being of light—appears before him. This being asks him a question, nonverbally, to make him evaluate his life and helps him along by showing him a panoramic, instantaneous playback of the major events of his life. At some point he finds himself approaching some sort of barrier or border, apparently representing the limit between earthly life and the next life. Yet, he finds that he

must go back to the earth, that the time for his death has not yet come. At this point he resists, for by now he is taken up with his experiences in the afterlife and does not want to return. He is overwhelmed by intense feelings of joy, love, and peace. Despite his attitude, though, he somehow reunites with his physical body and lives. (21–22)

Before Moody presents the accounts that flesh out the parts of this pattern, he issues several caveats which become important when we compare his findings to the description of the afterlife in the Bahá'í writings. No two experiences are the same. No single individual experiences all the parts of the model. No single part of the model occurs in every experience. The order of the parts of the model vary from one subject to another. The clarity of the experience increases in proportion to the length of time the subject is clinically dead. Not everyone who has been clinically dead can recollect experiencing an afterlife.

But perhaps Moody's most important remark prefatory to his presentation of the particular accounts in *Life After Life* is his statement qualifying the shortcomings of his sampling technique. His sampling is limited to those experiences which, in effect, support the pattern he had begun to observe. In the main body of this text he does not discuss or even mention those who had alternative experiences. In addition, Moody admits that his sampling is limited with regard to the number of people interviewed and to the lack of cross-cultural cases:

> In fact, one of the many reasons I say that my study is not "scientific" is that the group of individuals to whom I have listened is not a random sample of human beings. I would be very interested in hearing about the near-death experiences of Eskimos, Kwakiutl Indians, Navahos, Watusi tribesmen, and so on. (*Life After Life* 145)

Still another factor in the uniformly positive nature of these experiences, though Moody fails to note it, might be that the sample is taken from those who wished to talk about the experience. Though he mentions this in his succeeding study *Reflections On Life After Life*, people with negative experiences would obviously be less enthusiastic about sharing their story since a negative afterlife might seem to incriminate their performance in this life.

Moody organizes the life-after-death accounts into fifteen parts of an overall model. These begin with the initial stages in which one might hear his death pronounced by attending physicians, and they end with statements about how the afterlife experience affects the succeeding physical life of the revived subject. The resulting paradigm of the afterlife is positive and is corroborated at almost every turn by passages in the Bahá'í writings.

In the first part of the experience subjects describe the separation of the mind from the body and often view the body in its lifeless form:

> I was out of my body looking at it from about ten yards away, but I was still thinking, just like in physical life. And *where* I was thinking was about my normal bodily height. I wasn't in a body, as such. (Moody, *Life After Life* 50)

> I kept bobbling up and down, and all of a sudden, it felt as though I were away from my body, away from everybody, in space by myself. Although I was stable, staying at the same level, I saw my body in the water about three or four feet away, bobbling up and down. (*Life After Life* 35)

While nothing in the Bahá'í writings specifically describes the sensation of departing from the body, there are several passages, some of which have been cited in our previous discussion, that describe a similar relationship between the cognitive faculty (which is a property of the soul and, therefore, continuous) and the physical body. These passages indicate that since the soul is not attached to or dependent on the physical being, one does not cease to be cognitively aware after death:

> That a sick person showeth signs of weakness is due to the hindrances that interpose themselves between his soul and his body, for the soul itself remaineth unaffected by any bodily ailments. Consider the light of the lamp. Though an external object may interfere with its radiance, the light itself continueth to shine with undiminished power. In like

manner, every malady afflicting the body of man is an impediment that preventeth the soul from manifesting its inherent might and power. When it leaveth the body, however, it will evince such ascendancy, and reveal such influence as no force on earth can equal. (Bahá'u'lláh, *Gleanings* 154)

But the mind is the power of the human spirit. Spirit is the lamp; mind is the light which shines from the lamp. Spirit is the tree, and the mind is the fruit. ('Abdu'l-Bahá, *Some Answered Questions* 209)

the rational soul, meaning the human spirit, does not descend into the body—that is to say, it does not enter it, for descent and entrance are characteristics of bodies, and the rational soul is exempt from this. The spirit never entered this body, so in quitting it, it will not be in need of an abiding-place: no, the spirit is connected with the body, as this light is with this mirror. When the mirror is clear and perfect, the light of the lamp will be apparent in it, and when the mirror becomes covered with dust or breaks, the light will disappear.

. . . The personality of the rational soul is from its beginning; it is not due to the instrumentality of the body. . . . (*Some Answered Questions* 239–40)

These descriptions of the relationship of the body to the soul and of the continuity of consciousness after the death of the body do not allude to viewing the body as an inevitable part of the severing of the relationship between the body and the rational soul; but given the nature of the relationship as it is here depicted, we can readily accept the feasibility of such an experience.

A second parallel between the accounts in *Life After Life* and the discussions in the Bahá'í writings concerns the encounter with other souls shortly after the initial sensation of departure from the body. Moody's subjects describe a sense of comfort and companionship resulting from this experience. In most cases there is the specific recognition of other souls who had already passed on, individuals the subject had known in life:

I realized that all these people were there, almost in multitudes it seems, hovering around the ceiling of the room. They were all people I had known in my past life, but who had passed on before. I recognized my grandmother and a girl I had known when I was in school, and many other relatives and friends. It seems that I mainly saw their faces and felt their presence. They all seemed pleased. It was a very happy occasion, and I felt that they had come to protect or to guide me. . . . It was a beautiful and glorious moment. (*Life After Life* 55–56)

Several weeks before I nearly died, a good friend of mine, Bob, had been killed. Now the moment I got out of my body I had the feeling that Bob was standing there, right next to me. I could see him in my mind and felt like he was there, but it was strange. I didn't see him as his physical body. . . . He was there but he didn't have a physical body. (*Life After Life* 56)

I had the feeling that there were people around me, and I could feel their presence, and could feel them moving, though I could never see anyone. Every now and then, I would talk with one of them, but I couldn't see them. And whenever I wondered what was going on, I would always get a thought back from one of them, that everything was all right, that I was dying but would be fine. (*Life After Life* 58)

The Bahá'í writings describe essentially the same experience of recognizing deceased individuals, but with additional insights. There seems to be implicit in Bahá'u'lláh's descriptions a qualification for the soul that experiences the companionship of other departed souls or at least an indication of who the companions will be:

Blessed is the soul which, at the hour of its separation from the body, is sanctified from the vain imaginings of the peoples of the world. . . . The Maids of Heaven, inmates of the loftiest mansions, will circle around it, and the Prophets of God and His chosen ones will seek its companionship. With them that soul will freely converse, and will recount unto them that which it hath been made to endure in the path of God, the Lord of all worlds. (*Gleanings* 156)

Know thou that the souls of the people of Bahá, who have entered and been established within the Crimson Ark, shall associate and commune intimately one with another, and shall be so closely associated in their lives, their aspirations, their aims and strivings as to be even as one soul. (*Gleanings* 169–70)

From these statements by Bahá'u'lláh it would seem that only particular souls will experience companionship in the next life, souls which are "sanctified" and souls "of the people of Bahá." Furthermore, the companionship is depicted in more detail. The newly deceased will recount what they have accomplished and will converse with other spiritually eloquent souls. But in another passage from the Bahá'í writings it becomes clear that such an experience is not confined to people of one religion or to those who have attained all wisdom:

> As to the question whether the souls will recognize each other in the spiritual world: This (fact) is certain; for the Kingdom is the world of vision (*i.e.*, things are visible in it), where all the concealed realities will become disclosed. How much more the well-known souls will become manifest. The mysteries of which man is heedless in this earthly world, those will he discover in the heavenly world, and there will he be informed of the secret of truth; how much more will he recognize or discover persons with whom he hath been associated. ('Abdu'l-Bahá, *Tablets of Abdul-Baha Abbas* 1:205)

A third parallel between *Life After Life* and the Bahá'í writings concerns the panoramic review of one's life, an experience consistent with most of the subjects Moody interviewed. This review seems to be instigated by a nonverbal query from the "being of light," not with the aim of rebuking, but with the purpose of evaluating the subject's accomplishments and failures. According to most accounts, the purpose is to instruct lovingly:

> When the light appeared, the first thing he said to me was "What do you have to show me that you've done with your life?", or something to this effect. And that's when these flashbacks started. . . .
> Now, I didn't actually see the light as I was going through the flashbacks. He disappeared as soon as he asked me what I had done, and the flashbacks started, and yet I knew that he was there with me the whole time. . . . He was trying to show me something in each one of these flashbacks. It's not like he was trying to see what I had done—he knew already—but he was picking out these certain flashbacks of my life and putting them in front of me so that I would have to recall them.

. . . There wasn't any accusation in any of this, though. When he came across times when I had been selfish, his attitude was only that I had been learning from them, too. (*Life After Life* 65–67)

Bahá'u'lláh describes precisely the same procedure, not for one category of soul only, but for everyone:

It is clear and evident that all men shall, after their physical death, estimate the worth of their deeds, and realize all that their hands have wrought. (*Gleanings* 171)

Furthermore, since we never know when we ourselves shall be faced with this examination of our performance on earth, Bahá'u'-lláh commands us to evaluate our progress daily so that we might be prepared for a frank assessment at our life's end:

Bring thyself to account each day ere thou art summoned to a reckoning; for death, unheralded, shall come upon thee and thou shalt be called to give account for thy deeds. (*Hidden Words* 11)

In the accounts of the subjects in Moody's study, particularly in the accounts of those who seem to have had an extended experience, other parallels between *Life After Life* and the Bahá'í writings are evident. For example, all of Moody's subjects acknowledge the ineffable nature of their near-death experiences. They find language incapable of conveying the reality of that existence:

Now, there is a real problem for me as I'm trying to tell you this, because all the words I know are three-dimensional. As I was going through this, I kept thinking, "Well, when I was taking geometry, they always told me there were only three dimensions, and I always just accepted that. But they were wrong. There are more." And, of course, our world—the one we're living in now—*is* three-dimensional, but the next one definitely isn't. And that's why it's so hard to tell you this. I have to describe it to you in words that are three-dimensional. That's as close as I can get to it, but it's not really adequate. I can't really give you a complete picture. (*Life After Life* 26)

Bahá'u'lláh also indicates the indescribable difference between the two planes of existence, but He cautions that even were it possible to describe this difference, it would be unwise to do so:

> The nature of the soul after death can never be described, nor is it meet and permissible to reveal its whole character to the eyes of men. . . . The world beyond is as different from this world as this world is different from that of the child while still in the womb of its mother. (*Gleanings* 156–57)

Moody's subjects and the Bahá'í writings also agree on the purpose of the human soul, which is spiritual growth through learning, something Moody discusses more elaborately in his succeeding book, *Reflections On Life After Life*. One of Moody's subjects states that in the course of his experience he came to understand that according to the "being of light" the attainment of knowledge is the purpose of life:

> He seemed very interested in things concerning knowledge, too. He kept on pointing out things that had to do with learning, and he did say that I was going to continue learning, and he said that even when he comes back for me (because by this time he had told me that I was going back) that there will always be a quest for knowledge. He said that it is a continuous process, so I got the feeling that it goes on after death. (*Life After Life* 67–68)

We have already noted in the second chapter the emphasis in the Bahá'í writings on education as the purpose of physical reality. The Bahá'í definition of justice for the individual is to know and then to do. As we have also noted, the sort of knowledge and learning that is praised is that which leads to spiritual progress. In fact, Bahá'u'lláh states that the acquisition of knowledge is crucial if the soul is to fulfill its potential:

> Regard man as a mine rich in gems of inestimable value. Education can, alone, cause it to reveal its treasures, and enable mankind to benefit therefrom. (*Gleanings* 260)

In addition, there are many statements in the Bahá'í writings about the continuation of human learning in the next world.

Bahá'u'lláh states as a general principle that every soul will continue its progress after death:

> Know thou of a truth that the soul, after its separation from the body, will continue to progress until it attaineth the presence of God, in a state and condition which neither the revolution of ages and centuries, nor the changes and chances of this world, can alter. (*Gleanings* 155)

'Abdu'l-Bahá writes that, during such progress, the departed souls will discover the "mysteries of which man is heedless in this earthly world" (*Tablets of Abdul-Baha Abbas* 1:205).

Perhaps the most striking, and for our purposes the most significant, parallel between *Life After Life* and the Bahá'í writings is the similarity in tone between the description of total peace and joy which Moody's subjects experience, and the same sort of delight which the Bahá'í writings ascribe to the afterlife. All of Moody's subjects repeat that they did not want to return and do so only because they must or because they have an urgent sense of unfulfilled duty. All clearly would have preferred to stay in the afterlife:

> all I felt was warmth and the most extreme comfort I have ever experienced. (*Life After Life* 28–29)

> I began to experience the most wonderful feelings. I couldn't feel a thing in the world except peace, comfort, ease—just quietness. I felt that all my troubles were gone. . . . (*Life After Life* 29)

> As I went across the line, the most wonderful feelings came over me—feelings of peace, tranquillity, a vanishing of all worries. (*Life After Life* 75)

> I didn't want to go back, but I had no choice, and immediately I was back in my body. (*Life After Life* 76)

> When I had this wonderful feeling, there in the presence of that light, I

really didn't want to come back. But I take my responsibilities very seriously, and I knew that I had a duty to my family. So I decided to try to come back. (*Life After Life* 78)

This same sense of joy, exuberance, release, and transcendence is corroborated in numerous passages in the Bahá'í writings, but with a significant and consistent qualification:

Every pure, every refined and sanctified soul will be endowed with tremendous power, and shall rejoice with exceeding gladness. (Bahá'u'lláh, *Gleanings* 154)

Every soul that walketh humbly with its God, in this Day, and cleaveth unto Him, shall find itself invested with the honor and glory of all goodly names and stations. (*Gleanings* 159)

Know thou, of a truth, that if the soul of man hath walked in the ways of God, it will, assuredly, return and be gathered to the glory of the Beloved. (*Gleanings* 161)

They that are the followers of the one true God shall, the moment they depart out of this life, experience such joy and gladness as would be impossible to describe. . . . (*Gleanings* 171)

Unlike the implications of Moody's model, the Bahá'í writings specify a particular category of soul which experiences other-worldly delight. It is not just any soul but "every pure, every refined and sanctified soul," "every soul that walketh humbly with its God," "the soul of man that hath walked in the ways of God," and "they that are the followers of the one true God." These Bahá'í writings do not say that such qualifications deny a pleasant afterlife experience to souls who do not meet these qualifications, but other passages in the Bahá'í writings indicate that unpleasant afterlife experiences do await some souls. To have a valid understanding of the Bahá'í paradigm, therefore, we need to comprehend the basis for the negative afterlife experience.

Negative Afterlife Experiences

The unmistakably clear implication of Moody's *Life After Life* is that all alike receive a uniformly blissful experience in the afterlife. And yet such is not the case, because even a single alternative experience might indicate a whole other paradigm. Moody, in fact, acknowledges in his first work that at least one consistent alternative model exists. Relatively unnoticed in a final section on miscellaneous questions is a significant and unexpected observation by the author, a statement that those who had near-death experiences as the result of suicide seemed to have a uniformly negative experience:

> I do know of a few cases in which a suicide attempt was the cause of the apparent "death." These experiences were uniformly characterized as being unpleasant.
>
> As one woman said, "If you leave here a tormented soul, you will be a tormented soul over there, too." In short, they report that the conflicts they had attempted suicide to escape were still present when they died, but with added complications. In their disembodied state they were unable to do anything about their problems, and they also had to view the unfortunate consequences which resulted from their acts.
>
> A man who was despondent about the death of his wife shot himself, "died" as a result, and was resuscitated. He states:
>
>> I didn't go where [my wife] was. I went to an awful place. . . . I immediately saw the mistake I had made. . . . I thought, "I wish I hadn't done it."
>
> Others who experienced this unpleasant "limbo" state have remarked that they had the feeling they would be there for a long time. This was their penalty for "breaking the rules" by trying to release themselves prematurely from what was, in effect, an "assignment" —to fulfill a certain purpose in life. (*Life After Life* 143)

Moody's reference to an unpleasant limbo experienced because of "breaking the rules" has a profound impact on the entire implications of *Life After Life*. Clearly, not all models of the afterlife experience are positive and blissful. Furthermore, there does seem to be an important relationship between the physical performance and the afterlife experience, something quite the opposite of what Kübler-Ross implies by her statement that a Hitler and a Mother Theresa got the same treatment on death. Moody's observation about premature death even parallels the description in the Bahá'í writings of physical reality as a classroom, life as an "assignment," tests as fulfilling "a certain purpose in life," and the afterlife experience as a response to the evaluation of one's efforts.

In short, it would appear that assurance of an afterlife is by itself hardly a sufficient reason to relinquish a fear of death since few of us can be absolutely certain how well we have performed. The Bahá'í writings pointedly confirm the validity of such concern. In numerous passages the initial stages of a negative experience are described and the basis for such reward defined.

> they that live in error shall be seized with such fear and trembling, and shall be filled with such consternation, as nothing can exceed. (Bahá'u'lláh, *Gleanings* 171)

> The souls of the infidels, however, shall—and to this I bear witness —when breathing their last be made aware of the good things that have escaped them, and shall bemoan their plight, and shall humble themselves before God. They shall continue doing so after the separation of their souls from their bodies. (*Gleanings* 170–71)

> If it [the individual soul] be faithful to God, it will reflect His light, and will, eventually, return unto Him. If it fail, however, in its allegiance to its Creator, it will become a victim to self and passion, and will, in the end, sink in their depths. (*Gleanings* 159)

It would seem, in other words, that what Moody's subjects categorize as the consequences of "breaking the rules" might correspond to what Bahá'u'lláh designates in these passages with such epithets as "infidels," "they that live in error," and those who "become a victim to self and passion." And yet these phrases hardly seem appropriate to someone who, in despair, unwisely takes his life. Furthermore, it is not clear from these passages what exactly Bahá'u'lláh means by such phrases as "infidel." Certainly it would appear that to provide only two alternatives—one for the spiritually elite and another for failures—is only slightly more just and logical than for everyone to receive a uniformly blissful experience since, as we have noted previously, God's ultimate purpose for us is not judgment but education—to know and to worship Him. For while there seems to be some relationship between one's performance in the physical world and one's continued progress in the next life (and therefore some importance to physical life), it hardly seems appropriate that fallible souls should be condemned for an eternity for mistakes made over a relatively short period of time. Put another way, it seems improbable and inconsistent that a wise and just Deity would be incapable of making finer distinctions in judging us.

We can begin to see a more enhanced paradigm of the afterlife by examining what Moody himself discovered as he investigated further what had appeared only as an aberration of the model in his first work—the unpleasant experiences of the suicides. In *Reflections On Life After Life* Moody presents several distinct categories of afterlife experiences, all of which differ dramatically from the pattern he emphasizes in his initial study.

One such category is a variation on the "unpleasant limbo" model. This, too, is a negative experience, but it results from a sense of judgment that occurs during the panoramic replay. The subjects in this category do not seem to be in a negative environment or the sort of holding pattern described by those in the "unpleasant limbo" state. They appear to have committed enough negative acts, however, that the replay of their lives makes them feel immense shame and guilt:

> Then it seemed there was a display all around me, and everything in my life just went by for review, you might say. I was really very, very ashamed of a lot of the things that I experienced because it seemed that I had a different knowledge, that the light was showing me what was wrong, what I did wrong. And it was very real. (Moody, *Reflections* 34–35)

Moody himself speculates that a mode of experience most closely approximating the mythic hell of the Scriptures might be this same model as experienced by someone who had perpetrated horrendous acts upon others. Moody notes that his subjects were guilty of only minor transgressions and experienced great remorse. He surmises that were the emotions evoked by such a recounting proportionately greater for more grievous acts, there could be no worse punishment:

> If what happened to my subjects happened to these men, they would see all these things and many others come alive, vividly portrayed before them. In my wildest fantasies, I am totally unable to imagine a hell more horrible, more ultimately unbearable than this. (*Reflections* 38–39)

Of course, to experience such a hell depends on the spiritual sensitivity of the departed soul, something we cannot necessarily take for granted. If one is spiritually dead in this life and has become inured to guilt, it could be that such a one would remain oblivious after this life, at least for a certain duration. Another model Moody describes may well account for these heedless souls, as well as for those subjects in his first work who, while having experienced clinical death, could recall no afterlife experience. This is a realm of "bewildered spirits," a condition in which souls seem trapped between the physical and spiritual worlds of existence. According to accounts by Moody's subjects, these spirits seem dulled. They are physically dead but are still emotionally attached to the physical world:

> First, they state that these beings seemed to be, in effect, unable to surrender their attachments to the physical world. One man recounted that the spirits he saw apparently "couldn't progress on the other side because their God is still living here." That is, they seemed bound to some particular object, person, or habit. (*Reflections* 18)

Like the subjects who experienced the "unpleasant limbo," these souls were not doomed to dwell in a condition of bewilderment eternally; they were to be there only until they resolved whatever problem, difficulty, or attachment was keeping them in that perplexed state.

Unlike the subjects in the "unpleasant limbo," and unlike the subjects who experienced the guilt and shame during the panoramic replay, these "dulled spirits" do not seem to be in a state of guilt or regret; they are, instead, oblivious to what has happened to them, "not knowing who they are or what they are" (Moody, *Reflections* 20). They are between worlds, unable to return to the physical realm but uninterested in finding out what is in store for them, or else they are spiritually blind, unable to perceive the world of the spirit. Some even try "unsuccessfully to communicate with persons who were still physically alive" (*Reflections* 21).

With the enhanced portrait of negative afterlife experiences offered in *Reflections On Life After Life,* Moody dramatically alters the dominant impression created by his first work and gives a kind of empirical confirmation for the principles governing the unpleasant afterlife experiences mentioned in the Bahá'í writings. For example, Moody's evidence clearly demonstrates a relationship between one's conduct in the physical world and one's subsequent experience in the afterlife. The evidence also implies a more complex response to the individual life than the two-part division of a heaven and a hell. In fact, Moody correctly asserts that there is no reason to doubt that there are endless possibilities:

> I want very much for others to avoid taking my list of common elements as being a fixed, exhaustive model of what a near-death experience *must* be like. There is an enormously wide spectrum of experiences, with some people having only one or two of the elements, and others most of them. I anticipate that the list I have developed will be added to, modified, and reformulated. (*Reflections* 87)

Obviously we are extremely limited in what we can conclude from the data collected from "near-death" experiences. We may observe in these accounts some valid similarities with what we find set forth in the Bahá'í writings about the initial stages of our entrance into the next world; but since Moody's subjects all re-enter this life before they spend too much time in the afterlife, we can infer with certainty relatively little about what happens beyond their initial experiences. Nevertheless, Moody's additional categories of experience do support some important principles in the Bahá'í writings that serve to allay our fears and show us that spiritual progress beyond the physical world is possible.

The Relationship between Physical Action and Progress in the Afterlife

Perhaps the major Bahá'í principle supported by Moody's assertion of the possibility of an infinite variety of experiences is that there is operant in the next life a divine justice: we experience precisely what is appropriate to our individual spiritual condition at the time of our transition. Stated another way, God is not limited to certain predetermined categories of response for adjudging our success or failure and for preparing us for further growth. And since the object of our continued life is spiritual growth, we can assume that the judgment itself is somehow calculated to ensure our additional learning and development as human souls.

Moody's observations also support the Bahá'í concept of salvation as described in the paradigm in the second chapter. That is, there is no sense in Moody's accounts of a final point of development—salvation is an endless journey toward perfection. Viewed in terms of many traditional theological descriptions of the afterlife, this principle implies that there is no single point in the progress of the soul at which human development is finished. Advancement is always relative. No doubt the joy, release, and sense of fulfillment that is the initial lot of some souls would seem to be a veritable heaven; but 'Abdu'l-Bahá says that "as the perfections of humanity are endless, man can also make progress in perfections after leaving this world" (*Some Answered Questions* 237).

The Bahá'í teaching that learning and spiritual development continue after death is also supported in the accounts by Moody's subjects in their description of a "Vision of Knowledge," an afterlife experience in which "they got brief glimpses of an entire separate realm of existence in which all knowledge—whether of past, present, or future—seemed to co-exist in a sort of timeless state" (*Reflections* 9). Other subjects describe a moment of enlightenment when they seem to have complete knowledge. They describe the experience as a condition wherein they are aware of universal secrets, as if they were in a school or library where knowledge is readily available, where whatever they want to know is made suddenly accessible (*Reflections* 11–14).

We have already noted how the belief in the continued education and progress of the soul after death is likewise an essential part of the Bahá'í paradigm. But there are also numerous passages which similarly extol life after death as a reality in which learning will become accelerated because the verities that are concealed in this life will be apparent in the "realm of vision" ('Abdu'l-Bahá, *Selections* 176):

> Consider how a being, in the world of the womb, was deaf of ear and blind of eye, and mute of tongue; how he was bereft of any perceptions at all. But once, out of that world of darkness, he passed into this world of light, then his eye saw, his ear heard, his tongue spoke. In the same way, once he hath hastened away from this mortal place into the Kingdom of God, then he will be born in the spirit; then the eye of his perception will open, the ear of his soul will hearken, and all the truths of which he was ignorant before will be made plain and clear. ('Abdu'l-Bahá, *Selections* 177)

Another Bahá'í principle ostensibly reflected in the accounts of Moody's subjects has to do with grace and pardon in the next life. This principle of forgiveness is expressed in a variety of ways in the Bahá'í writings. For example, Bahá'í law forbids suicide, and Moody's subjects consistently report negative results attached to that act. And yet we can infer from a tablet of 'Abdu'l-Bahá to a bereaved widow that hope is not lost for such a soul:

> That honorable personage has been so much subjected to the stress and pain of this world that his highest wish became deliverance from it. . . . Thus it is seen that some, under extreme pressure of anguish, have committed suicide.
>
> As to him rest assured; he will be immersed in the ocean of

pardon and forgiveness and will become the recipient of bounty and favor. ('Abdu'l-Bahá, in Bahá'u'lláh and 'Abdu'l-Bahá, *Bahá'í World Faith* 378–79)

It may well be that this individual experienced an initial "unpleasant limbo" before being comforted by the "ocean of pardon and forgiveness"—the purpose of God, after all, is to educate. But the passage suggests that the ultimate destiny of a suicide is not to be wretched, but to be nurtured and assisted.

The assurance that every soul continues to grow after death also has a more weighty significance. It means that growth is possible not only for those souls who have an initially positive experience but also for some souls who have entered the next life in some sort of sinful state and yet desire to become transformed. A negative condition may endure for a period, but change and progress are still possible, perhaps even probable. 'Abdu'l-Bahá writes that all movement of the soul in the afterlife is progressive:

All creation, whether of the mineral, vegetable or animal kingdom, is compelled to obey the law of motion; it must either ascend or descend. But with the human soul, there is no decline. Its only movement is towards perfection; growth and progress alone constitute the motion of the soul. (*Paris Talks* 89)

In the world of spirit there is no retrogression. The world of mortality is a world of contradictions, of opposites; motion being compulsory everything must either go forward or retreat. In the realm of spirit there is no retreat possible, all movement is bound to be towards a perfect state. (*Paris Talks* 90)

Taken singly and out of context, then, these passages from the talks of 'Abdu'l-Bahá might seem to imply that no matter what we do in our physical life, we are ultimately destined to progress. However, other portions of 'Abdu'l-Bahá's statements reveal the possibility of the soul's decline after death:

Know that nothing which exists remains in a state of repose—that is to say, all things are in motion. Everything is either growing or declining. . . .

Thus it is established that this movement is necessary to existence, which is either growing or declining. Now, as the spirit continues to exist after death, it necessarily progresses or declines. . . . ('Abdu'l-Bahá, *Some Answered Questions* 233)

In that same discussion 'Abdu'l-Bahá clarifies the nature of the soul's decline when He states, "In the other world to cease to progress is the same as to decline. . . . " (*Some Answered Questions* 233). For, according to 'Abdu'l-Bahá, a soul who is "deprived of these divine favors, although he continues after death, is considered as dead by the people of truth" (*Some Answered Questions* 225).

To understand further the principle of the soul's progress and decline, we can consider what 'Abdu'l-Bahá states about the progress of the soul in general. He affirms that all souls begin in a state of equality but soon become differentiated from one another by virtue of their efforts:

As for what is meant by the equality of souls in the all-highest realm, it is this: the souls of the believers, at the time when they first become manifest in the world of the body, are equal, and each is sanctified and pure. In this world, however, they will begin to differ one from another, some achieving the highest station, some a middle one, others remaining at the lowest stage of being. (*Selections* 171)

As we noted in the second chapter, God has "singled out for His special favor the pure, the gem-like reality of man, and invested it with a unique capacity of knowing Him and of reflecting the greatness of His glory" (Bahá'u'lláh, *Gleanings* 77). Bahá'u'lláh states further that God "hath endowed every soul with the capacity to recognize the signs of God" (*Gleanings* 106). And yet as we also noted, Bahá'u'lláh says in the Kitáb-i-Aqdas that recognition is not sufficient unless we act in accordance with that understanding: "These twin duties are inseparable. Neither is acceptable without the other" (*Synopsis* 11).

Hence, according to Bahá'u'lláh, every soul has a chance at progress, but that progress is still dependent on some sort of effort, some manner of employing free will: "Success or failure, gain or loss, must, therefore, depend upon man's own exertions. The more he striveth, the greater will be his progress" (Bahá'u'lláh, *Gleanings* 81–82). Logically, then, it is crucial to examine the role free will plays in the development of our souls after the death of our bodies.

Free Will and Progress in the Afterlife

Given that a soul's motion in the next world is always forward, stagnation is equivalent to regression. We have seen that a soul which has not fulfilled its potential may be as if it were dead compared to the souls which have developed. The question then arises as to whether such a soul is doomed to remain in that condition, whether the physical life is the only part of our development wherein we have the opportunity willfully to affect our own salvation. In short, can the soul initiate its own progress in the next life? If it can, how does it accomplish such a change?

The Bahá'í principles governing the progress of the soul in the afterlife seem occasionally misunderstood. Obviously we cannot progress through physical action in the next world. That inextricable metaphorical relationship between knowledge and deed as we have delineated it in chapter 3 no longer exists, or else it becomes markedly changed. No doubt we still recall the physical analogues from our earthly lives, but it is clear from the Bahá'í writings and is implied in the so-called afterlife experiences that in the next life we no longer have to struggle to perceive truth. Apparently spiritual reality and knowledge of that reality are no longer veiled in metaphorical disguise:

> When the human soul soareth out of this transient heap of dust and riseth into the world of God, then veils will fall away, and verities will come to light, and all things unknown before will be made clear, and hidden truths be understood. ('Abdu'l-Bahá, *Selections* 177)

In such a context, we may presume that life's purpose will be apparent to all, or at least to all who have sufficiently developed spiritual faculties to perceive it. In such a context there would no longer be much merit in being able to discern the existence or validity of spiritual verities since this insight would be the property of all alike. Because we must assume that there is also no physical expression of learning, how then might the soul strive? What can it *do* to foster its own advancement if *doing* implies action? And if there is no physical action to perform, can the soul in such a state truly be said to have free will?

It is abundantly clear in numerous passages in the Bahá'í writings (and corroborated by Moody's work) that the soul once dissociated from the body is not merely an amorphous entity oblivious to its own identity, urged along by forces beyond its control and understanding. The soul after the physical life has the selfsame identity it had in the physical world and can initiate thought and action, albeit not physical action.

However, one often cited passage from the writings of 'Abdu'l-Bahá might at first glance seem to refute the soul's ability to think and act. In speaking of how a soul progresses in the next life, 'Abdu'l-Bahá states that we can advance by three processes: "through the bounty and grace of the Lord alone, or through the intercession and the sincere prayers of other human souls, or through the charities and important good works which are performed in its name" (*Some Answered Questions* 240). Without other statements by 'Abdu'l-Bahá that explain quite clearly what "bounty and grace" involve and how we participate in receiving forgiveness, this passage could be taken to mean that the soul is powerless. It is dependent for its advancement on the prayers or deeds of those still in the physical world, or else on the unpredictable intervention of a Deity Who may or may not decide to help out. In such an interpretation, the soul is presumed to have no ability to influence its own salvation once it has become dissociated from the body.

To believe that the soul is powerless with regard to its development in the hereafter is hardly comforting. Such a view conveys an image of the afterlife as a realm of mechanical entities. Furthermore, such an interpretation implies that the physical life is the focal point of existence, the exclusive part of one's life in which any vital or dramatic activity occurs. The afterlife, in such a context, would serve only to register the success with which the physical experience has been carried out.

But in other passages 'Abdu'l-Bahá makes it clear that the soul in the next world can communicate with others, can pray for other souls, and, if it has died in sin, can also instigate its *own* progress:

> As we have power to pray for these souls here, so likewise we shall possess the same power in the other world, which is the Kingdom of God. Are not all the people in that world the creatures of God? Therefore, in that world also they can make progress. As here they can receive light by their supplications, there also they can plead for forgiveness and receive light through entreaties and supplications. (*Some Answered Questions* 232)

We can hardly fail to recognize that to supplicate, to plead, to make entreaties are actions that require free will on the part of those who have died in sin. The capacity to do this is due to the "bounty and grace of the Lord alone," but so, for that matter, is all progress man makes at every stage of existence. As the discussion of the paradigm of physical reality demonstrates in the second chapter, human advancement, whether individually or collectively, inevitably depends upon the bounty of God. For example, were it not for His grace and bounty, God would not continue to send the Manifestations in spite of the mistreatment they receive from the world of humanity.

When we misinterpret these passages from the statements of 'Abdu'l-Bahá to imply that physical existence is the one opportunity for growth, or at least for the soul to take an active part in its own development, we fail to recognize that other forms of volitional activity can abound in a spiritual realm. Furthermore, by perceiving the willful progress of the soul as confined to the physical stage of life, we fail to recognize that the forgiveness of God is not so confined. Perhaps there remains in the next world the requisite that we desire pardon and grace and act accordingly in order to receive His forgiveness, but certainly we can envision other sorts of action besides physical activity to accomplish this—meditation and prayer, for example.

In order to appreciate the logic and distinctive nature of the Bahá'í paradigm of the afterlife and its relationship to the physical life, we must recognize that we can initiate our spiritual growth in both worlds. Certainly there is a significant and indisputable emphasis in the Bahá'í writings on the utilization of the physical life to ensure spiritual growth. Indeed, we are repeatedly cautioned about the awesome dangers of not taking advantage of this crucial opportunity for development and are further admonished that the physical experience will not be repeated and offers unique opportunities for our betterment. At the same time we should not mistakenly regard the physical life as the only occasion for our development or even necessarily as the focal point of our eternal existence.

In Gloria Faizi's *The Bahá'í Faith: An Introduction,* for example, we find a passage which might be taken to imply that the end of the physical life is the end of our opportunity to strive for enlightenment and growth:

> We should therefore pay constant attention to our spiritual growth now because it will be too late when our life here is over, and any blessings which we may then receive will be dependent on the grace of God alone rather than on what we could have earned by our own efforts in this life. (Faizi 56)

One might infer from Faizi's explanation that in the afterlife there is no will, no independence of thought, no way to express the desire to progress. Such an inference would seem to be corroborated by 'Abdu'l-Bahá's statement that it is "possible" that the condition of a sinner may become changed in the next world, but only through God's mercy:

> It is even possible that the condition of those who have died in sin and unbelief may become changed—that is to say, they may become the object of pardon through the bounty of God, not through His justice—for bounty is giving without desert, and justice is giving what is deserved. (*Some Answered Questions* 232)

The fact is, however, that even in the physical life we do not "earn" our progress—as we have already noted, all progress depends on God's bounty. Likewise, we have noted that, while God is "Ever-Forgiving," without our free request for assistance, we may not receive His bounty.

Since the spiritual principles at work in the physical realm reflect the reality of the spiritual realm, it may well be that the same requisite persists into the next world, making this forgiveness dependent on our action in that realm. It may be that the penitential process depicted by Bahá'u'lláh whereby a sinner can receive grace is as appropriate to the afterlife as it is to this life:

> When the sinner findeth himself wholly detached and freed from all save God, he should beg forgiveness and pardon from Him. . . . The sinner should, between himself and God, implore mercy from the Ocean of mercy, [and] beg forgiveness from the Heaven of generosity. . . . (*Tablets of Bahá'u'lláh* 24)

To be "freed from all save God" might be an easy task in an afterlife where God's ascendancy is apparent. Yet this one requisite, that the sinner himself initiate the process, has implications of tremendous importance since we know that in the next life it is incumbent on the soul to recognize its failures and deficiencies and to request assistance.

We might wonder who would *not* choose to be assisted, given the operation of such benign principles. Yet in our physical lives we observe those who fail to recognize blatantly obvious spiritual principles. But more to the point, we also encounter those who recognize and accept the validity of certain spiritual verities but refuse to abide by their dictates. It is conceivable, then, that such obstinacy could persist into the next life. And while we cannot even speculate about the ultimate destiny of such souls, it is possible that, like Milton's Satan, such a one could remain stubbornly proud or willful or perverse in spite of retaining the opportunity for reformation.

Bahá'u'lláh's exhortation to His mischievous half-brother Mírzá Yaḥyá offers an excellent example of one who failed to respond to God's forgiveness. In spite of Mírzá Yaḥyá's willful attempts to kill the Manifestation, to usurp the authority of Bahá'u'lláh, and to destroy the Bahá'í Faith itself, Mírzá Yaḥyá was told by Bahá'u'lláh in the Kitáb-i-Aqdas that forgiveness was readily available to him if he would but seek it. Bahá'u'lláh states that he should "fear not because of thy deeds," asks him to "return unto God, humble, submissive and lowly," and promises that "He will put away from thee thy sins," concluding that "thy Lord is the Forgiving, the Mighty, the All-Merciful" (qtd. in Shoghi Effendi, *God Passes By* 170). Since repentance and forgiveness are private acts, possibly Mírzá Yaḥyá did effect the process of his own salvation, if not in this life, then in the next. The point is that the modern notion of iniquity as environmentally caused, while in keeping with the Socratic notion that no one does evil in full knowledge, is at odds with the Bahá'í concept that one can know and still do wrong. The human soul is not merely a computer registering the sum total of external influences. There is a will, which, we are told, persists into the next life.

In *Memorials of the Faithful* 'Abdu'l-Bahá recounts that when the degree of Mírzá Yaḥyá's rebellion became apparent, Bahá'u'-lláh's brother Mírzá Músá tried to persuade Mírzá Yaḥyá to "mend his ways" (88), thinking that if Mírzá Yaḥyá only understood what he was doing, he would desist in his attacks and change his attitude. After repeated attempts to reconcile his brother to Bahá'u'-lláh, Mírzá Músá realized that the problem was not Mírzá Yaḥyá's failure to understand the truth but his refusal to respond to it:

> Day and night he tried to make him mend his ways, but all to no avail. . . . Even then he never ceased trying, thinking that somehow, perhaps, he could still the tempest and rescue Mírzá Yaḥyá from the gulf. His heart was worn away with despair and grief. He tried everything he knew. At last he had to admit the truth of these words of Saná'í:

> > If to the fool my lore you'd bring,
> > Or think my secrets can be told
> > To him who is not wise—
> > Then to the deaf go harp and sing,
> > Or stand before the blind and hold
> > A mirror to his eyes. (*Memorials* 88)

We must presume, in other words, that through willfulness a wayward soul can choose to stray irretrievably from God's bounty.

Two passages demonstrate this principle in vivid terms. 'Abdu'l-Bahá explains that a wayward soul may be revived, but not against its will—there must be recognition and acceptance followed by the request for assistance:

> If a soul remains far from the Manifestation, he may yet be awakened; for he did not recognize the manifestation of the divine perfections. But if he loathe the divine perfections themselves—in other words, the Holy Spirit—it is evident that he is like a bat which hates the light.
>
> This detestation of the light has no remedy and cannot be forgiven—that is to say, it is impossible for him to come near unto God. This lamp is a lamp because of its light; without the light it would not be a lamp. Now if a soul has an aversion for the light of the lamp, he is, as it were, blind, and cannot comprehend the light; and blindness is the cause of everlasting banishment from God. . . .
>
> The meaning is this: to remain far from the light-holder does not entail everlasting banishment, for one may become awakened and vigilant; but enmity toward the light is the cause of everlasting banishment, and for this there is no remedy. (*Some Answered Questions* 127–28)

We can, then, conceive of a soul willfully refusing to turn toward the light, in this life or the next, and thereby rejecting its own redemption.

In another passage 'Abdu'l-Bahá amplifies the possibility of eternal banishment (self-imposed though it be) and implies the process by which such a soul might falter and fail:

> But on the other hand, when man does not open his mind and heart to the blessing of the spirit, but turns his soul towards the material side, towards the bodily part of his nature, then is he fallen from his high place and he becomes inferior to the inhabitants of the lower animal kingdom. In this case the man is in a sorry plight! For if the spiritual qualities of the soul, open to the breath of the Divine Spirit, are never used, they become atrophied, enfeebled, and at last incapable; whilst the soul's material qualities alone being exercised, they become terribly powerful—and the unhappy, misguided man, becomes more savage, more malevolent than the lower animals themselves. All his aspirations and desires being strengthened by the

lower side of the soul's nature, he becomes more and more brutal, until his whole being is in no way superior to that of the beasts that perish. Men such as this, plan to work evil, to hurt and to destroy; they are entirely without the spirit of Divine compassion, for the celestial quality of the soul has been dominated by that of the material. ('Abdu'l-Bahá, *Paris Talks* 97)

Here 'Abdu'l-Bahá is concerned primarily with the status of a soul in this life, but we can infer that a soul thus diverted from its just or proper course of development might possess a similar incapacity in the afterlife.

By analogy, if a child in the womb of its mother had the ability to choose how it would develop, and if it decided not to grow limbs or develop senses and other tools essential for successful advancement in the physical environment, it might be born into this life incapable of existing beyond the level of a plant relative to its full capacity as a human being. Furthermore, such a one would be incapable of discerning its own inadequacies and degraded condition because it would be oblivious to its own nature and incapable of acquiring such knowledge. Similarly, were we to enter a spiritual environment devoid of spiritual faculties and sensibilities, we might not know where to turn for assistance or even be aware that we needed help.

In light of the possibility of such a condition, we can imagine that without some merciful intervention of God, such a soul could, like a planet slipped from orbit, follow the dictates of its own centrifugal momentum, its own willfulness and ignorance. Unchecked, such a one could become so remote from the magnetic attraction of God's love that it might fly irretrievably into remoteness.

Whatever fear we may have of death, therefore, is not the dread of nonexistence or of God's justice, but a concern for our own response to God's laws and their unrelenting consequence in our lives. This concern is well illustrated by a story about the Hand of the Cause of God Ṭarázu'lláh Samandarí. As he lay dying, he requested that a prayer for steadfastness be read. A Bahá'í attending him, fully aware of the exemplary life of service and devotion Mr. Samandarí had lived, asked why of all people he should feel the need for that particular prayer. The reply was, "There is still time."*

Since there is still time for each of us, we can never completely relinquish the care with which we attend that daily assessment of our progress, for in large part the greatest mystery in the whole process is ourselves. The laws of God are constant, unchanging, just, and without caprice or guile. God is, from a Bahá'í perspective, ever ready to meet our needs, but we are faced with one stark and unremitting truth—we are stuck with ourselves eternally. We cannot in this life or the next become someone else or dissociate ourselves from our own consciousness. It is precisely as Hamlet feared.

The Bridge between Two Worlds: The Purpose Fulfilled

Perhaps the most significant contribution of the Bahá'í writings to an understanding of the relationship between our physical lives and our experience in the next life is a lucid portrayal of how the soul associates with the body. We have already discussed in the second chapter certain aspects of the subtle relationship between body and soul. But as we pull together the major inferences we can derive from our study, we come to focus on one overriding conclusion about our physical lives: Every aspect of our life in the temporal realm is geared to our birth into the next stage of our existence. To study the way in which the soul associates with the body is to appreciate more completely the pervasive methods by which this life is precisely geared to prepare us for the continuation of life in a totally different environment.

'Abdu'l-Bahá uses several revealing analogies in order to explain the subtle connection between soul and body. For example, He states that the connection is like that of a bird to a cage:

---

*I do not know where I first heard the story about Mr. Samandarí, though it sounds like a story told by Winston Evans, who traveled with Mr. Samandarí while Mr. Samandarí was visiting the United States.

> To consider that after the death of the body the spirit perishes is like imagining that a bird in a cage will be destroyed if the cage is broken, though the bird has nothing to fear from the destruction of the cage. Our body is like the cage, and the spirit is like the bird. . . . Its feelings will be even more powerful, its perceptions greater, and its happiness increased. . . . That is why with utmost joy and happiness the martyrs hasten to the plain of sacrifice. (*Some Answered Questions* 228)

'Abdu'l-Bahá's analogy is comforting not only because it portrays death as a release, but also because it demonstrates with such ease the fact that the soul, though associating with the body, is in no way dependent on the body for its existence. Not that the relationship between the body and soul is unimportant—if we have discovered anything in this venture, it is the existential imperative that we scrutinize daily the subtle, pervasive, and, in this physical life, inextricable relationship between the body and soul.

The point is that the soul is fully capable of development even when its relationship with the physical body is terminated or rendered ineffectual through disease, retardation, or other means. 'Abdu'l-Bahá clarifies this further with another analogy:

> But when the body is wholly subjected to disease and misfortune, it is deprived of the bounty of the spirit, like a mirror which, when it becomes broken or dirty or dusty, cannot reflect the rays of the sun nor any longer show its bounties. (*Some Answered Questions* 229)

'Abdu'l-Bahá goes on to explain that, though the instrumentality of the body no longer exists, the soul's light still shines, however undetected by those in the presence of the physical person.

A contemporary analogy might serve well to clarify further the relationship between the body and the soul. A television receiver is, by itself, of little worth. Even if plugged in, turned on, and pulsing with the life which electricity mysteriously bestows upon its myriad transistors and circuitry, the receiver is in no way alive or useful until there are unseen and otherwise undetectable signals for the receiver to translate into visible form and audible sound. Conversely, the waves of the soul may be existent, full of vital messages. But without the instrumentality of the body through which the soul can communicate, we are prevented from any sort of effective understanding of that ethereal energy. We are deprived of that companionship.

When the soul can no longer communicate through the instrumentality of the body because of the body's dysfunction, the relationship is severed. As yet in our understanding of this process we are unable to determine exactly at what point the severance occurs. We might deduce from the research of Moody and others that the separation can be temporary. Modern medicine seems to have sanctioned the detection of brain waves as the index of whether the body is yet a fit vehicle for the type of life we classify as distinctly human.

Whatever the truth may be about the instant at which dissociation occurs, another corollary point is worth noting. The nature of the body-soul relationship as portrayed in 'Abdu'l-Bahá's analogies vindicates the feeling expressed by so many elderly that in their minds and thoughts they are as young as they ever were. After all, it is not the signal that is aging—it is the capacity of the receiver to transmit the signal well.

If the soul is unaffected by the deterioration of the body, we should, indeed, view the transition from this world to the next as a positive experience, as a birth and not a death. Dr. Hossain B. Danesh, in his monograph *The Violence-Free Society* (34–35), describes how he presents death as a positive experience to terminally ill children in order to counsel and console them. The basis for his description is a comparison of mortal life to the period of gestation in the womb, an analogy used by Bahá'u'lláh (*Gleanings* 157) and 'Abdu'l-Bahá (*Some Answered Questions* 198). The parable portrays several children in the womb speculating with consternation what has become of a sibling who has just been born. In a delightful reflection on the variety of views we have about death, the children remaining in the womb consider what fate has befallen their departed sibling. Of course, from our point of view, and, it is hoped, from the perspective of the child being counseled, we can laugh at the needless fears of these infants: soon they will begin a life infinitely more glorious than what they leave behind, and just as soon they will be reunited with their loved one.

The analogy thus serves to demonstrate two of the most important issues about the relation of the physical life to our eternal existence, and about the purpose of physical reality in general. First, the analogy reveals concretely and effectively that birth into the next life, though a fearful and dramatic transition like physical birth, is a positive event, an expansion of life rather than a diminution. Second, the analogy demonstrates the point we have already repeatedly noted—that physical life is intended to be a concerted training for another life, not incidental to it, just as the gestation period is a relatively meaningless existence except as it provides the opportunity for the child to develop tools for life in the physical world.

Dr. Danesh's simple but weighty conceit also appropriately returns us to where we began—starkly realizing our own limited appreciation of the way in which our physical lives prepare us for the life we will all soon enter. For just as we might long to reassure our own unborn children about the immense love we stand waiting to bestow on them, so we may sense in the words of the Manifestations the same attempt at loving reassurance and confirmation: "Were men to discover the motivating purpose of God's Revelation, they would assuredly cast away their fears. . . . " (*Gleanings* 175).

Mike and Nancy Samuels, the authors of a recent pediatrics book, give additional weight to Dr. Danesh's metaphor with an observation about the world of the womb. They note that our attempts to communicate love and affection while the child is yet in the womb are actually felt by the infant, even though these expressions of love can but hint at the more direct expressions which are to follow after birth (*Well Baby Book* 61). In the same way, we can only vaguely intimate the love that awaits us.

Perhaps the most important observation the Samuels make relevant to our discussion is their description of how completely every aspect of the environment of the unborn child prepares it for its functioning in the physical world:

> From the moment of conception the baby's destiny as a human being propels it onward. Truly the baby is meant to live its life outside, not inside, the womb. The womb is simply a temporary shelter for the

baby until it is capable of making its way in the outside world. (*Well Baby Book* 90)

The authors go on to note that the serenity of the mother at birth and the continued connection with the mother for the first days and weeks after birth "form a bridge which links the baby's two worlds" (*Well Baby Book* 91). Here we cannot help noting the metaphorical parallel between the bond uniting mother and child and the physical and spiritual sustenance provided us by God through the Manifestations and through the whole metaphorical classroom. This spiritual bond nurtures us in our infancy, ushers us lovingly from our temporary shelter into our eternal abode:

> The Prophets and Messengers of God have been sent down for the sole purpose of guiding mankind to the straight Path of Truth. The purpose underlying their revelation hath been to educate all men, that they may, at the hour of death, ascend, in the utmost purity and sanctity and with absolute detachment, to the throne of the Most High. (Bahá'u'lláh, *Gleanings* 156–58)

Like divine midwives, the Manifestations bend every effort toward preparing us for our departure from the Kingdom of Names and our birth into a spiritual realm, a world of vision where the realities we have struggled so hard in this life to understand will be clear and apparent. Since knowledge will be available to all and since deeds as we understand them in physical terms will no longer be available to us, we cannot even guess at the rest of the paradigm for that reality, how spiritual progress will take place, or what "faith" will involve. But whatever the principles for progress operant in the afterlife, we have arrived at one stark and unremitting truth in our quest to understand the spiritual purpose of physical reality. The more we understand and utilize the spiritual process devised for our progress in this life, the easier will be our birth pangs and the better equipped we will be in the life beyond to continue our eternal spiritual journey.

Bibliography

Bibliography

'Abdu'l-Bahá. *Bahá'í Prayers*. See Bahá'u'lláh, the Báb, and 'Abdu'l-Bahá, *Bahá'í Prayers*.

————. *Bahá'í World Faith*. See Bahá'u'lláh and 'Abdu'l-Bahá, *Bahá'í World Faith*.

————. *The Divine Art of Living*. See Bahá'u'lláh and 'Abdu'l-Bahá, *The Divine Art of Living*.

————. *The Individual and Teaching*. See Bahá'u'lláh, 'Abdu'l-Bahá, and Shoghi Effendi, *The Individual and Teaching*.

————. *Memorials of the Faithful*. Translated by Marzieh Gail. Wilmette, Ill.: Bahá'í Publishing Trust, 1971.

————. *Paris Talks: Addresses Given by 'Abdu'l-Bahá in Paris in 1911*. 11th ed. London: Bahá'í Publishing Trust, 1969.

————. *The Promulgation of Universal Peace: Talks Delivered by 'Abdu'l-Bahá during His Visit to the United States and Canada in 1912*. Compiled by Howard MacNutt. 2d ed. Wilmette, Ill.: Bahá'í Publishing Trust, 1982.

————. *Selections from the Writings of 'Abdu'l-Bahá*. Compiled by the Research Department of the Universal House of Justice. Translated by a Committee at the Bahá'í World Centre and Marzieh Gail. Haifa: Bahá'í World Centre, 1978.

————. *Some Answered Questions*. Compiled and translated by Laura Clifford Barney, 5th ed. Wilmette, Ill.: Bahá'í Publishing Trust, 1981.

————. *Tablets of Abdul-Baha Abbas*. 3 vols. New York: Bahai Publishing Society, 1909–16.

————. "The Worst Enemies of the Cause Are in the Cause." *Star of the West* 6 (24 June 1915): 43–45.

The Báb. *Selections from the Writings of the Báb*. Compiled by the Research Department of the Universal House of Justice. Translated by Habib Taherzadeh et al. Haifa: Bahá'í World Centre, 1976.

Bahá'u'lláh. *Epistle to the Son of the Wolf*. New ed. Translated by Shoghi Effendi. Wilmette, Ill.: Bahá'í Publishing Trust, 1953.

————. *Gleanings from the Writings of Bahá'u'lláh*. 2d ed. Translated by Shoghi Effendi. Wilmette, Ill.: Bahá'í Publishing Trust, 1976.

————. *The Hidden Words of Bahá'u'lláh*. Translated by Shoghi Effendi. Wilmette, Ill.: Bahá'í Publishing Trust, 1939.

————. *Kitáb-i-Íqán: The Book of Certitude*. 2d ed. Translated by Shoghi Effendi. Wilmette, Ill.: Bahá'í Publishing Trust, 1950.

————. *The Proclamation of Bahá'u'lláh to the Kings and Leaders of the World.* Haifa: Bahá'í World Centre, 1967.

————. *The Seven Valleys and The Four Valleys.* 3d ed. Translated by Ali-Kuli Khan and Marzieh Gail. Wilmette, Ill.: Bahá'í Publishing Trust, 1978.

————. *A Synopsis and Codification of the Kitáb-i-Aqdas: The Most Holy Book of Bahá'u'lláh.* [Compiled by the Universal House of Justice.] Haifa: Bahá'í World Centre, 1973.

————. *Tablets of Bahá'u'lláh Revealed after the Kitáb-i-Aqdas.* Compiled by the Research Department of the Universal House of Justice. Translated by Habib Taherzadeh et al. Haifa: Bahá'í World Centre, 1978.

Bahá'u'lláh and 'Abdu'l-Bahá. *Bahá'í World Faith: Selected Writings of Bahá'u'lláh and 'Abdu'l-Bahá.* 2d ed. Wilmette, Ill.: Bahá'í Publishing Trust, 1976.

————. *The Divine Art of Living: Selections from the Writings of Bahá'u'lláh and 'Abdu'l-Bahá.* Compiled by Mabel Hyde Paine. Revised by Anne Marie Scheffer. Wilmette, Ill.: Bahá'í Publishing Trust, 1986.

Bahá'u'lláh, 'Abdu'l-Bahá, and Shoghi Effendi. *The Individual and Teaching: Raising the Divine Call.* Compiled by the Research Department of the Universal House of Justice. Wilmette, Ill.: Bahá'í Publishing Trust, 1977.

Bahá'u'lláh, the Báb, and 'Abdu'l-Bahá. *Bahá'í Prayers: A Selection of Prayers Revealed by Bahá'u'lláh, the Báb, and 'Abdu'l-Bahá.* New ed. Wilmette, Ill.: Bahá'í Publishing Trust, 1982.

Boethius, Anicius. *The Consolation of Philosophy.* New York: Modern Library, 1943.

Braga, Joseph, and Laurie D. Braga. See Elisabeth Kübler-Ross, *Death: The Final Stage of Growth.*

Bunyan, John. *The Pilgrim's Progress.* New York: Oxford Univ. Press, 1984.

Chadwick, Henry. "Christianity Before the Schism of 1054." *Encyclopædia Britannica: Macropaedia.* 1974 ed.

Chaucer, Geoffrey. *The Complete Poetry and Prose of Geoffrey Chaucer.* Edited by John H. Fisher. New York: Holt, 1977.

Danesh, Hossain B. "The Violence-Free Society: A Gift for Our Children." *Bahá'í Studies* 6 (Oct. 1979).

Faizi, Gloria. *The Bahá'í Faith: An Introduction.* Rev. ed. Wilmette, Ill.: Bahá'í Publishing Trust, 1972.

Gordis, Robert. *The Book of God and Man: A Study of Job.* Chicago: Univ. of Chicago Press, 1965.

Graham, Billy. "My Answer." *Tampa Tribune* 1 Apr. 1982: B3.

The Holy Bible: Revised Standard Version. New York: Thomas Nelson, 1953.

Kübler-Ross, Elisabeth. *Death: The Final Stage of Growth.* Englewood Cliffs, N.J.: Prentice, 1975.

————. "Dr. Kübler-Ross: Go Gently into that good night." *Tampa Times* 19 Apr. 1977: B1.

Kushner, Harold S. *When Bad Things Happen to Good People.* New York: Avon, 1981; repr. 1983.

Milton, John. *The Complete Poetical Works of John Milton.* Edited by Douglas Bush. Boston: Houghton, 1965.

Moody, Raymond A., Jr. *Life After Life.* New York: Bantam, 1975; repr. 1976.

————. *Reflections On Life After Life.* New York: Bantam, 1977.

Muḥammad. *The Koran.* Translated by J. M. Rodwell. New York: Dutton, 1953.

Nabíl-i-A'ẓam [Muḥammad-i-Zarandí]. *The Dawn-Breakers: Nabíl's Narrative of the Early Days of the Bahá'í Revelation.* Translated and edited by Shoghi Effendi. Wilmette, Ill.: Bahá'í Publishing Trust, 1932.

Plato. *The Republic of Plato.* Translated by Francis Macdonald Cornford. New York: Oxford Univ. Press, repr. 1958.

Pollock, Selton. "God and a Heretic." In *The Dimensions of Job: A Study and Selected Readings.* Edited by Nahum N. Glatzer. New York: Schocken, 1969.

Pope, Alexander. *An Esssay on Man.* Excerpted in *The Norton Anthology of English Literature.* Edited by M. H. Abrams et al. 2 vols. 4th ed. New York: Norton, 1979. Vol. 1, pp. 2243–50.

Popper, Karl R. "The Spell of Plato." *The Open Society and Its Enemies.* 2 vols. 5th rev. ed. Princeton, N.J.: Princeton Univ. Press, 1966. Vol. 1.

Richards, I. A. *The Philosophy of Rhetoric.* The Mary Flexner Lectures on the Humanities. London: Oxford Univ. Press, 1936.

Samuels, Mike, and Nancy Samuels. *The Well Baby Book.* New York: Summit, 1979.

Schaefer, Udo. *The Light Shineth in Darkness: Five Studies in Revelation after Christ.* Translated by Hélène Momtaz Neri and Oliver Coburn. Oxford: George Ronald, 1977.

Shakespeare, William. *The Complete Works of Shakespeare.* Edited by Hardin Craig. Chicago: Scott, 1951.

Shoghi Effendi. *The Advent of Divine Justice.* Wilmette, Ill.: Bahá'í Publishing Trust, 1984.

————. "Excerpts from Letters of the Guardian to Assemblies and Individual Believers." *Bahá'í News,* no. 210 (Aug. 1948): 2–3.

————. *God Passes By.* New ed. Wilmette, Ill.: Bahá'í Publishing Trust, 1974.

————. *High Endeavours: Messages to Alaska.* Compiled by the National Spiritual Assembly of the Bahá'ís of Alaska. N.p.: National Spiritual Assembly of the Bahá'ís of Alaska, 1976.

Simpson, Louis. *An Introduction to Poetry.* New York: St. Martin's, 1967.